Florida
at Sea

Florida at Sea

A MARITIME HISTORY

JOE KNETSCH, NICK WYNNE
AND ROBERT REDD

THE
History
PRESS

Published by The History Press
Charleston, SC
www.historypress.com

Front cover, clockwise from top left: Naval Amphibious Training Base Fort Pierce. *Courtesy of the Wynne Collection*; A lighthouse along the Florida Atlantic Coast. *Courtesy of the Wynne Collection*; TASCO, a Tampa shipyard. *Courtesy of the Wynne Collection*; An aerial view of the shipping container port in Miami, Florida. *Library of Congress*; A small steamer on the Ocklawaha River. *Courtesy of the Wynne Collection*.
Back cover, top: Vintage postcards. *Courtesy of the Florida Historical Society*; *inset*: *Concho*, the ship that would take the Rough Riders to Cuba. *Courtesy of the Joe Knetsch Collection*.

First published 2023

Manufactured in the United States

ISBN 9781467154109

Library of Congress Control Number: 2022950055

Notice: The information in this book is true and complete to the best of our knowledge. It is offered without guarantee on the part of the authors or The History Press. The authors and The History Press disclaim all liability in connection with the use of this book.

CONTENTS

INTRODUCTION

Although Ponce de Leon has been generally credited as the first European to "discover" Florida in 1513, recent scholarship presented by Todd Turrell, Robert Carr and Brian Schmitt in their 2019 book *The Florida Keys: A History Through Maps* argues strongly that the discovery of Florida and early mapping efforts began in 1500, more than a decade before the de Leon landing. In 1500, Juan de la Cosa created the first map of the Florida Peninsula, while a second map, the Cantino Planisphere, was created in 1502, followed in 1511 by a map by Peter Martyr. Although generally describing lands north of Cuba and the Bahamas, these maps existed before de Leon's so-called discovery. While these early maps are generally vague about some well-known features of today's maps of Florida, they do provide outlines of the coasts of Florida, including several major bays, usable harbors and river mouths. Given the rough terrain and the hostile populations of Indigenous peoples, it would take more than three centuries before the interior of the peninsula would be entirely mapped.

These early maps provided enough information to encourage Spanish authorities to allow expeditions to create outposts and settlements. De Leon followed his early exploration with a second voyage along the Gulf of Mexico coast in 1521, but he abandoned his efforts after being wounded in a confrontation with local tribes. His failed effort was followed seven years later by an expedition led by Pánfilo de Narváez. It, too, was unsuccessful. A third expedition in 1539, led by Hernando de Soto, was more successful, but de Soto's quest for gold and riches led him out of the Florida Peninsula through several modern southern states. Finally in 1559, Tristán de Luna y Arellano led a successful expedition to the Pensacola Bay area, but tragedy befell the small community of Santa María de Ochuse when a hurricane destroyed it and most of the supply ships in the bay. After spending two years at a small settlement inland, the surviving colonists packed up and headed home. The area was not resettled until 1698. St. Augustine, founded in 1565, became the principal Spanish settlement in Florida.

The Spanish began to strengthen St. Augustine, but it was little more than a military outpost that existed to provide a safe haven for Spanish treasure ships and as an operations hub for Catholic priests who created a vast network of missions that eventually stretched from present-day South Carolina across South Georgia to the northern tier of the peninsula.

The interior of the peninsula remained unsettled and unexplored, a pattern that extended into the British colonial period and continued during the early years of the American territorial and statehood periods. From Bayport on the Gulf Coast to New Smyrna on the Atlantic Coast, an imaginary line defined the principal areas of settlement. North of this line, small farms and large plantations flourished, while a few isolated farms and ranches existed to the south. The absence of roads, the threat of violence by Native Americans and the rugged topography prevented movement into the interior. Although the threat of violence by Native Americans ended with the Third Seminole War in 1857, it would take some years before roads would be built and the harsh environment conquered.

In the territorial and antebellum periods, the Florida economy depended on small ports, as they provided homes for the hundreds of ships that transported the major crops to market. Cotton, tobacco and cattle were sent to international markets via such ports as Apalachicola, Fernandina and New Smyrna, while Key West, located at the very tip of the Florida Keys, provided protection and supplies for transports sailing down the coasts of the peninsula, bound for distant ports. Along the St. Johns River, small schooners collected products from farms and plantations and ferried them to Cow Ford, present-day Jacksonville, and Mayport, where they could be transferred to larger oceangoing vessels. The construction of the Florida Railroad, which ran from Fernandina to Cedar Key and was finalized in 1860, promised northern Florida planters and farmers a faster, more efficient way to get their crops to ports and off to European markets. The outbreak of the Civil War in 1861 ended this promise temporarily, but operations quickly resumed at war's end. Once peace was restored, Florida agriculturalists found that a considerable change had occurred in their markets. European markets, so vital in the antebellum period, were replaced by northern markets as the Industrial Revolution gathered steam—markets that could be served directly through rail connections.

In the post–Civil War period, however, ports became even more critical to Florida's people as the population grew rapidly. Large-scale settlement of the interior became a reality with the development of steamboats that could ply rivers at will, carry large loads of supplies and essential goods and transport large numbers of passengers in relative comfort. New industries, such as citrus production and fishing, were dependent on fast transportation to out-of-state markets, and several failed efforts were made to shorten the time from farm to market through the construction of canals across the peninsula.

Three factors played important roles in Florida's postwar growth: (1) the full implementation of the Homestead Act, which made acquiring land easier; (2) the expansion of railroads connecting more ports and small towns; (3) and the rapid development of a burgeoning tourism industry, which stressed Florida flora and fauna, as opposed to the twentieth-century emphasis on beaches and sunshine.

Following the end of the Civil War, the United States found itself a major player in international affairs. Any nation that could muster the two largest armies in the world and supply them was a power to be reckoned with. The Monroe Doctrine, long dormant, suddenly took on a critical importance as the United States took a new interest in affairs in Latin and South America. Colonialism, long pursued by European nations in Africa and Asia, was forbidden in the Western Hemisphere, where America claimed hegemony. Old-style colonialism of conquer and occupy was replaced by a new American version of economic conquest and periodic military involvement to put down unrest or replace unfriendly governments. Because of its strategic location, Florida became an integral part of the neo-colonial efforts of the United States, and its ports became essential to military campaigns in the Americas. Key West and Pensacola became major supply harbors for naval expeditions to the south, while Mayport at the mouth of the St. Johns provided support for the United States' Atlantic operations along the coast.

In all stages of the settlement of Florida, water has played a decisive role. From small ports to large harbors, from rivers to creeks, from lakes to lagoons, water routes have been essential to Florida's development as a commercial, recreational, agricultural and cultural entity.

The objective of this book is to examine Florida's maritime history and look at the effect using maritime resources has had on the evolution of the people who have occupied the peninsula. As a result, the authors have paid considerable attention to the economic factors driving the need for maritime facilities. Given the word limitations placed on the authors, we can offer only a brief look at various aspects of this history. Some important events that occurred are mentioned only in passing, but the authors encourage readers to explore these on their own.

All mistakes in this book are regrettable and can be blamed on the authors. Enjoy!

Nick Wynne
Robert Redd
Joe Knetsch

1

THE MARITIME HISTORY OF COLONIAL FLORIDA

*M*ost people know the formal origins of colonial Florida as a Spanish colony based on the "discovery" of La Florida by Juan Ponce de Leon. Early maps of the peninsula may look ridiculous to modern eyes, but they were more accurate than we assume today. The entire southern portion south of the greater Tampa region might have been under water or flooded when de Leon made his voyages, and many of the islands depicted on the early Spanish maps may well have been just that—*islands*. We know from the descriptions of later explorers that during the rainy season in South Florida, the land is, indeed, often covered with water. As late as the 1840s, U.S. deputy surveyor Sam Reid noted in his letters to the surveyor general that the land below the Manatee River was covered with water and impossible to survey. Colonel Reid had the great advantage of having already surveyed some of the area, of leading expeditions to find live oaks and cedars along the coasts and swamps and guiding military units in the region during the Second Seminole War. How could the earlier mapping be so different? Colonel Reid had been on the ground, while the first maps generated by the Spanish were charted from ships in the Gulf or along the Atlantic Coast. Given the distances from the shallow coastlines Spanish vessels had to keep because of the ships' deep drafts, the location of the ships relative to the land and the crude compasses of the day, it is remarkable that early maps were as useful as they were.

Early Spanish explorers recorded their journeys and mapped new regions as guides for those who would certainly come after them. Spanish conquest in the "New World" was fueled by desires to spread Catholicism, find new sources of riches and exercise military power through conquest. They had little knowledge of how many Native peoples inhabited the regions and even less knowledge of their cultures and beliefs. The Spanish brought the "tools of the trade" of conquest—metal armor, steel swords, firearms and horses—as well as familiar foods and animals from home. Hogs, cattle, many new fruits and assorted European/North African grains were essential components for every expedition, and so, too, were diseases for which the aboriginal inhabitants had no resistance. The First Peoples of the New World were totally unprepared to face such an onslaught.

When the Spanish first began to explore the shores and rivers of Florida, they were greeted by Native people—Caloosa, Ayes, Tequesta, Tocabag and others—who traveled in long, dugout canoes, some over thirty feet in length and able to hold up to twenty or more people. Some of the Native Americans with larger canoes traded with their native counterparts in Cuba and possibly Hispaniola, and there is some evidence that trade routes with Mexico and Central America also existed. Recovered deposits of large caches of flint, which is not found in Florida, and some metal arrowpoints, also not found in Florida, indicate that the Native Americans in Florida traded with other tribes along the Mississippi River and its tributaries. Ideas and concepts were also traded, as evidenced by the similarities in the types of construction of ceremonial mounds.

Spanish narratives described some of the larger canoes as having sails or being propelled by large paddles handled by the passengers. The canoes were the workaday carriers of trade goods and people. As Susan Parker noted, "Canoes with their maneuverability, shallow draft and slim hulls could negotiate the short and tortuous course between the St. Johns and the St. Marys." They could also be used often in times of heavy rains and overflows that would ground other types of craft. Most of these canoes drew less than a foot of water, thus making them invaluable during rainy, wet seasons.

Many of the Florida tribes also used coracles, or skin/hide boats, to transport goods across bodies of water. In 1897, Frank Hamilton Cushing found evidence that catamarans were used by the Caloosa tribe in the Marco Island area of modern Collier County. Jonathon Dickinson recorded their use by the local Ais Indians along the Indian River region of the eastern coast of Florida. The use of the dugout canoes, catamarans, coracles and other types of vessels indicates the range of Native American craftmanship and innovation. The exchange of ideas and goods by Native tribes preceded the arrival of Europeans and had been going on for centuries.

Early explorations of Florida started immediately after the first Europeans arrived. Catholic priests looking to convert the Indigenous people or

Pedro Menéndez de Avilés established the first permanent European settlement at St. Augustine in North America in 1565. St. Augustine was a military bastion created to offer protection for Spanish fleets plying the Gulf Stream. *Courtesy of the St. Augustine Historical Society.*

adventurers searching for gold generally confined their explorations to the coasts or to the dry lands of northern Florida and actually attempted to penetrate the interior. Only a few, like Álvaro Mexía, deliberately set out to explore and map useable waterways and passages along the eastern coast of the colony. His 1605 expedition of the Atlantic Coast carefully noted the rivers and creeks that flowed to the ocean, as well as Native villages and encampments. The Tomoka River and the nearby village of Nocoroco were among his important discoveries. Farther south, Mexía found the village of Surruque located at Turtle Mound, in today's Canaveral National Seashore. At the foot of the oyster shell mound, he discovered a launching area for canoes capable of going out into the ocean and possibly trading with the inhabitants of the Bahamas. The village of Caparaca, near Spruce Creek and the Halifax River, was another Timucuan settlement with a large burial mound of sand and shell and was considered by Mexía to be a major governing center of the Timucuans, who dominated the area. Knowledge of these villages and others in the vicinity was important for the Spanish, since their yearly treasure fleets plied the nearby Gulf Stream and information about any potential threat to them was essential.

Threats to Spain were not restricted to the ocean. The English had established their first colonies in lands north of Spanish Florida, which extended as far north as present-day South Carolina, and were aggressively pushing southward as more and more colonists came to North America. The English recruited Native Americans warriors as proxy soldiers and armed them with flintlocks, which gave them an advantage over the tiny Spanish garrisons and converted Guale Indians at the missions. Slowly, but inexorably, Spanish priests were forced to abandon the missions they had established as more and more territory was occupied by English settlers.

Guale was the northernmost province of Spanish Florida and included the islands along the coast as far north as Edisto Island, South Carolina. Considered an essential buffer zone between the English and the Spanish in St. Augustine, the province was a source of trouble for Spanish authorities, and several Indian revolts against Spanish control occurred during the seventeenth century. Constant interference by the English, as well as some by the French, culminated in the expulsion of the Spanish in 1684 following the capture of the missions at Guadalquini (St. Simons) and Santa Catalina (St. Catherines) Islands by an English-sponsored Indian force armed with flintlocks.

The new governor of Florida, Juan Márquez Cabrera, vowed to stabilize the situation in Guale province and to revitalize the colony with new settlers from the Canary Islands. The Crown agreed in principle with Cabrera's plan but required the mapping of the king's possessions in Florida before he would agree to the final release of the Canary Islanders for settlement. Alonso Solana, who had traveled extensively in the colony, was chosen to complete the mapping, but his completed map was more like a sketch of the territory and did not give the Crown what it had asked for since it was not an accurate depiction of the lands or settlements. As historian Luis Arana noted, it may not have given the Spanish king what he desired, but it gives us an idea of the limited amount of knowledge the Spanish had of their land after over one hundred years of ownership.

This limited knowledge hampered commerce and travel in the interior of Florida for the Spanish, who lacked even a rudimentary knowledge about waterways along the coastal regions of their territory. Spanish control of Florida was challenged not only by the English colonists to the north but also by an increasingly aggressive French presence in Louisiana. In an effort to strengthen their claims of ownership of the peninsula and to be prepared for military action if needed, the Spanish authorities dispatched Don Francisco Maria Celi, a naval captain, to explore and map the western coast of Florida. His explorations of the Tampa Bay area, the first such expedition since that of Pánfilo de Narváez in 1528, showed that the area around the bay and up the Hillsborough River was suitable for settlement although no European nation had done so. Before Spanish authorities could make use of this information, Spain was forced to cede Florida to the British in 1763 at the end of the Seven Years' War.

The only area of Florida that was completely mapped was the region immediately surrounding St. Augustine and extending northward up the coast to Fernandina. Much of this information came as a result of James Edward Oglethorpe's invasion of Florida in 1740 and the failed Spanish retaliatory raid into southern Georgia by Governor Manuel de Monteano in 1742.

During the first two hundred years of Spanish occupation, Florida was considered little more than a military outpost offering protection and a safe haven for Spanish fleets plying the Gulf Stream with cargoes from Latin and South America. Little money or efforts were invested in attracting more settlers to serve as a bulwark against the expansionist French and English colonists to the north. Despite the lack of interest by the authorities in exploiting the resources of the peninsula, small industries and areas did develop. One of the more unusual examples of colonial trade routes during the early years of Spanish occupation was the development of trade of foodstuffs and manufactured goods between the Apalachee Indians and Cuba. The center of this trade was the Mission San Luis, at the center of rich agricultural lands so productive that the Apalachee could supply most of the food requirements for themselves and the Spanish population of St. Augustine and still have a sizeable surplus. This surplus foodstuff was loaded on small canoes and carried to the small port at San Marcos on Apalachee Bay, where waiting ships took it to Havana. San Luis residents included several shipowners who regularly exported Apalachee agricultural products to Havana in exchange for items from around the world.

Fishing rancheros along the western coast of Florida that supplied the growing Havana market were established, and so, to, were cattle ranches around modern Gainesville. Indeed, as Charles Arnade noted in his research of the early cattle industry, these cattle ranches supplied St. Augustine with beef. He also speculated that there may have been an illegal trade from the great ranch at "La Chua" down the Santa Fe River into the Suwannee River and out to Havana. Much of this trade ended with a revolt in 1702 in Timucua against the cattle ranches when many of the ranchers were killed by the Natives and the cattle driven off into the hinterland.

In 1702, James Moore, the governor of British Carolina, launched a series of attacks aimed at conquering St. Augustine and destroying the Spanish mission system in Florida. When his siege of St. Augustine failed, Moore, along with his Creek Indian allies, redirected his attacks toward the agriculturally rich Apalachee Province. By 1706, Mission San Louis and the other Spanish missions had been destroyed or abandoned. Nearly eight thousand Apalachees were taken to the Carolinas to work as slaves for the plantations of that region, and the raids by Moore's troops ended the illegal trade with Havana.

The English took control of Florida in 1763 at the end of the Seven Years' War in exchange for returning Havana, which it had captured, to Spanish control. The English period, which lasted for only twenty-one years or until the end of the American Revolution, when it was returned to Spanish control, was an era of speculation and opportunity for those willing to brave the dangers of swamps, diseases and possibly hostile Native populations. Land grants were given to prominent Englishmen, who quickly established plantations to grow indigo, rice and tobacco. Two of the most famous of these were the New Smyrna Colony and Rollestown, both of which were social experiments for helping the poor and unemployed of Europe.

The New Smyrna Colony, owned by Andrew Turnbull and two partners, was situated along the shores of the Mosquito Inlet near the mouth of the Tomoka River. Turnbull recruited workers from the island of Minorca, who eventually revolted against the restrictions imposed by Turnbull's overseers and fled to St. Augustine. Despite the turmoil, the Turnbull colony left an indelible mark on present-day New Smyrna and the surrounding area. Rollestown was located along the shores of the St. Johns River in present-

Above: European settlers in colonial Florida who claimed lands outside St. Augustine faced a lonely existence and the daily danger of Indian attacks. As a result, few Spanish colonists ventured far from the protection of soldiers stationed at the fortress of Castillo de San Marcos. *Courtesy of the Lewis N. Wynne Collection, hereafter referred to as the Wynne Collection.*

Left: James Moultrie served as lieutenant governor (twice) and governor of Florida during the British colonial period. He was an opponent of Andrew Turnbull in matters relating to the administration of British Florida. *Courtesy of the Wynne Collection.*

day East Palatka. Denys Rolles, the proprietor, recruited laborers from the slums of London, and Rollestown soon gained a reputation as the home of disreputable and undisciplined settlers. Other plantations, modeled on those in the former British colonies to the north, flourished. Indeed, Florida became a sanctuary for American colonists who supported the British cause during the American Revolution. When the Revolution ended, control of Florida passed from British hands into those of the previous owner, Spain.

Spain had refused to leave what maps it had to the new occupants of Florida, which meant that the English had to explore and map the peninsula on their own. The English wasted little time in appointing William Gerard de Brahm as

General Patrick Tonyn served as the last governor of British Florida from 1774 until 1783. As governor, Tonyn offered refuge to Loyalist colonists who fled northern colonies during the American Revolution and to the Minorcans who fled Andrew Turnbull's New Smyrna Colony. *Courtesy of the Wynne Collection.*

surveyor general for the southern colonies. Although the eccentric de Brahm was difficult to work for and with, he was an excellent surveyor and an accomplished cartographer. His early survey of the eastern coast of Florida proved to be accurate. De Brahm also undertook to survey many of the land grants given by the king along the coast and up the St. Johns River. To assist him, he did not hesitate to hire other competent surveyors, such as Bernard Romans. Although they eventually wound up as competitors, their combined works gave the English accurate information about their new colony. The maps and surveys created by de Brahms and Romans made it possible to establish viable inland trade networks and safer passages for ships carrying goods to and from the new colony. De Brahm's book *The Atlantic Pilot* set the pattern and is still used today for ships sailing along the coasts of North America.

The most accurate surveyor during the English period, however, was George Gauld. Gauld was formerly a schoolmaster in the navy aboard the HMS *Preston*. There he served as a teacher of mathematics and learned all he could about surveying the coasts along the various islands of the Mediterranean Sea, a skill that would bring him a modicum of fame. The governor of West Florida, George Johnstone, realized that no reliable maps

These rocks are all that remain of the wharf constructed by workers at the Turnbull Colony in New Smyrna. Because of their isolation south of St. Augustine, colonists depended on ships to bring in supplies and to take the indigo, rum and sugar they produced to markets. *Courtesy of Dorothy Moore and Roger T. Grange.*

or charts of the waters included in his new jurisdiction were available and that the colony's development would be set back without more accurate information. To remedy this situation, he called for an immediate survey of the territory, and in 1764, Gauld got the assignment.

He boarded the HMS *Tartar* for a voyage to Pensacola, which was to be his home base for a number of years. By happenstance, one of the passengers on this voyage was William Harrison, the son of John Harrison, a clockmaker whose timepieces would revolutionize navigation. William had been entrusted by his father with a clock designed for maritime use that was taken aboard the *Tartar* for a final test of the accuracy in establishing longitude. The tests were successful, and the lessons learned about calculating this vital measurement were not lost on George Gauld. His new job would soon require him to use the clock in determining geographic coordinates and to record them on his charts. Gauld's subsequent charts and measurements were remarkable and were so accurate they were not supplanted as the official charts of the coast until long after his death. His maps of the Florida Keys were so reliable that the U.S. Coast and Geodetic Survey retained his charts and changed them only after major storms had altered the islands or created new passages between them.

Most of the vessels used by Gauld while conducting his surveys had shallow drafts. The main surveying ship, the *Northampton*, which carried the supplies, replacement parts and other baggage, did not draw more than six and a half to seven feet. Anything more would have been too great to cross the bars of most of the inlets he charted. Smaller surveying boats drew even less water and made them useful for the shallow depths of most of the western coast of Florida and the Keys, too.

The careful work of the men who charted the waters of Florida carried over into the work on their land grants. Many of these maps show that along the St. Johns River, the surveyors frequently recorded what type of craft could navigate up to the property's waterfront. The John Broward grant survey, for example, noted that a small sloop could navigate up to the existing dock. This type of precise information made it convenient for shippers and growers to understand what was needed to get their crops or lumber to the market.

The lumber trade in East Florida prospered during the English ownership. The lands along the St. Marys River were heavily forested naturally with live oak and longleaf pine. Long rafts of lumber were floated down the river to the town of St. Marys, where they were gathered for further shipment. Tracts of timber were often listed in Wilbur H. Siebert's *Loyalists in East Florida*, which includes examples of compensation claims made by British colonials following the transfer of Florida back to the Spanish in 1784. The British government, with its large navy, purchased large quantities of timber and naval stores for planking, masts and waterproofing. Colonials who provided these critical supplies were among the wealthiest settlers in British Florida.

The Siebert collection is also valuable for enumerating the type of crops grown and shipped, the number and species of livestock and the value of buildings possessed by colonists at the time of the transfer back to Spain in 1784. Benjamin Springer, a prosperous colonist, listed "A small Schooner, several Flat Boats & Canoes," which he valued at £100 in his claim. Springer also included crops of rice and indigo "of the first quality…200 head of grown hogs…[and] 50 head of Horses." Alexander Paterson noted in his claim that although his family lived in St. Augustine, he also cultivated a small plantation with fifty acres enclosed and produced annual crops of Indian corn. Claimants also requested compensation for slaves, personal possessions and businesses. Of the £647 million requested in claims, British colonists received only about £170 million in compensation, and most of that went to recipients of large grants. Nevertheless, the large value of the claims made demonstrates how well Florida's economy had flourished under British control.

When the English left Florida in 1783–84, they took with them what they could and sold the rest to the incoming Spanish. And like the Spanish before them, they left few maps of the interior of the territory for the newcomers to use. Although they had lost possession of Florida, the British continued to be a force to be reckoned with in their former colony. So poor was the state of the Spanish economy in Florida that the English firm of Panton and Leslie was allowed to control the trade with the Native populations along the border and into Alabama, Mississippi and southwestern Georgia. Trade agreements made with Florida Creeks and Seminoles gave them the opportunity to foment difficulties for the Spanish and for the Americans in the southern states. For the next two decades, British provocateurs exploited the inability of the Spanish in St. Augustine and Pensacola to pacify these tribes and to bring stability to the peninsula.

East Florida did not attract the numbers of Spanish settlers that could readily build defenses against either potential Indigenous enemies or intrusions from northern neighbors. The Miccosukee in northern Florida frequently raided settlements along the St. Johns and took cattle and captives for ransom. Their random attacks from land and water filled the settlers on the frontier with fear, and small outposts like Picolata or Fort Pupa did little

The Pensacola headquarters of the British trading company Panton-Leslie, which controlled the commerce with Florida's Indians during the Second Spanish Colonial Period. Panton-Leslie played an important role in the continued British efforts to create chaos on the Georgia-Florida frontier. *Courtesy of the Wynne Collection.*

to deter these Native raiders. Frequent attacks by Americans from across the Georgia border added to an even greater sense of insecurity. The Americans were looking for cattle and slaves for their farms and plantations or pursuing Native Americans who had raided their holdings. Over the course of the next few decades, the near state of war was a constant on this most violent of frontiers. Conditions did not encourage settlement, and Florida languished in the hot tropical sun, poor, neglected and frequently deadly.

The obvious weakness of Spanish efforts in controlling their reclaimed province encouraged adventurers like William Augustus Bowles to ignore Spanish authorities and create their own state. Bowles, with the secret support of the British military, created the "State of Muskogee" and proclaimed himself as the head of state. With a small force of some four hundred men, he conducted raids against the Spanish for several years. Eventually captured and transported to Spain, he managed to escape and returned to Florida. Once again, he mounted raids against the Spanish, and with the help of some of his Indian allies, Bowles raided and took control of the Panton and

Leslie trading post on the St. Marks River. Captured a second time in 1803, Bowles was imprisoned in Havana and died there in 1805. The weakness of the Spanish rule in Florida opened the way for further intrigue by the British as the tensions grew between the United States and the British in the post–Revolutionary War period.

Americans, too, had a covetous eye on Florida. In 1812, a group of Georgians, led by John Houston McIntosh, occupied Amelia Island and the busy port of Fernandina. With the aid of a small fleet of American gunboats, they forced the Spanish commandant to surrender Fort San Carlos, a small outpost on the island, and the town to them. Immediately, these co-called Patriots proclaimed the creation of a new republic, the Republic of East Florida; called for support from a detachment of American troops; and marched on St. Augustine to demand its surrender. Federal authorities, alarmed by the direct participation of American troops and the possibility of a war with Spain at a time when its relationship with Great Britain was deteriorating, hastily recalled the American troops and entered into negotiations with Spanish colonial officials for the return of the occupied territory in 1813. Just a year later, General Buckner Harris of Georgia attempted to create another government, independent of Spanish control, at Payne's Town, south of present-day Gainesville. This, too, ended in failure.

In Europe, conflict between Great Britain and the revolutionary government of France threatened to erupt into a world war. Americans, grateful for the support of the French and the Spanish during the Revolutionary War, sympathized with the French and continued to do so after Napoleon Bonaparte seized control of the French government and proclaimed himself emperor. Following the purchase of the Louisiana Territory from a cash-strapped French government in 1803, an act viewed as decidedly pro-French by the British, relations between Great Britain and its former colonies deteriorated rapidly. The British navy, which had gained almost complete control of the high seas following the defeat of the French navy at Trafalgar in 1805, sought to use its dominance to force the United States into a subservient position. Impressment of American sailors into the British navy, the passage of the Orders in Council attempting to limit American trade with Europe and conflicts as the United States pushed westward and northward to occupy its newly purchased territory created an atmosphere of increasing tensions between the two nations—tensions that would eventually lead to war in 1812.

The dysfunctional nature of Spanish governance in Florida and its weak military posture presented Great Britain with an opportunity to create difficulties for both the Spanish on the peninsula and Americans in the southern border states. So, too, did the sparsely settled lands of the northwestern states, where British provocateurs armed Native American tribes and encouraged them to make war on American settlers in Michigan, Ohio, Indiana and Illinois. Using these tribes as surrogate soldiers, frequently aided by British advisors, the frontiers of the United States were in constant turmoil. Seeking to unite the entirety of Native American tribes against the United States, British agents persuaded the Shawnee headman Tecumseh and his brother to venture south to persuade their Creek cousins in Alabama and Georgia to join a united effort to expel the upstart Americans from the frontier.

The Lower Creeks disagreed with this proposal, while the Upper Creeks, or Red Stick Creeks, joined the movement. This clash within the Creek Confederation caused a civil war among the factions. American intervention, led by Andrew Jackson, ended the idea of a unified Native American opposition at Battle of Horseshoe Bend in 1814. When the Red Stick faction lost, many of the survivors fled south into Florida, already home to the Miccosukee and Seminole Indians, who opposed American expansion into Florida. After the Battle of New Orleans, British interaction with the Native Americans of Florida lessened. The final blow to British involvement came in 1818 with the summary execution of two British agents by General Andrew Jackson following his invasion of Florida in pursuit of Creek Indians and runaway slaves. Not only did Jackson's invasion end British involvement, but it also paved the way for the American purchase of Florida in 1819 when Spain acknowledged that it could not properly govern the province or prevent Indian raids against Americans. A declining colonial power with limited resources, Spain had other, more profitable possessions that demanded these resources, and it wasn't willing to go to war with the United States to protect its claims of sovereignty.

Florida was now an American territory, and unlike the Spanish rule, American possession saw the development of a cash-crop economy based on slavery and the rapid settlement of the upper half of the peninsula. Settlers came from all the southern states, bringing with them complete households, livestock and slaves. It was, said one wag, "as if the whole state of Virginia moved lock, stock and barrel to the Florida wilds."

American possession of Florida also saw the nation's involvement in three Indian wars that were not concluded until 1857. The longest wars ever fought by the United States, the Seminole Wars produced the first truly

Andrew Jackson led American forces against the Red Stick Creeks in a series of frontier battles. He invaded Spanish Florida twice—in 1814 and 1818—which led to the Adams-Onis Treaty transferring ownership of the peninsula to the United States. *Courtesy of the Wynne Collection.*

accurate maps of the Florida interior by the U.S. Army, which carefully noted the size and location of most rivers, lakes and springs. Armed with the knowledge gained about these critical resources, American settlers quickly exploited them.

2

TERRITORIAL FLORIDA,
INDIAN WARS AND STATEHOOD

From the earliest days of English colonization in North America, relations with Spanish authorities in Florida had always been difficult, stemming primarily from the Spaniards' failure to control the Native American tribes. As English colonists pushed farther south, they accused the Spanish of encouraging these tribes to carry out raids against English settlements, capturing livestock, murdering colonists and stealing African American slaves. In addition, the Indians and the Spanish provided safe havens for runaway slaves fleeing the plantations and farms of Georgia and the Carolinas. This displeasure with the failure of Spanish authorities continued after the successful American Revolution, although Spain was an ally. During the War of 1812, Andrew Jackson, the primary military commander for American forces in the South, defeated a large force of Creek Indians at the Battle of Horseshoe Bend in March 1814. Following this battle, he pursued remnants of the group into Florida, where Spanish and British military units provided supplies and safety.

By November 1814, Jackson had invaded the province; forced Spain's ally, Great Britain, to evacuate its military forces by capturing Pensacola; and pursued them to Mobile and New Orleans. Although Jackson was successful in defeating the British there in January 1815 and despite the end of formal war between the two powers, British meddling in Indian affairs in Florida continued. As a result, conflict continued between American settlers and Native Americans across the border with Spanish Florida.

The exact cause for and date of the beginning of the Seminole Wars in Florida are debated among scholars, and there seems to be no definitive

Although most of the original inhabitants of Spanish Florida went with them to Cuba when the British took possession of the peninsula in 1764, their place was quickly taken by members of the Creek tribe who fled to Florida as American settlers pushed south with their farms and plantations. Neamathla led his band of Red Stick Creeks in battles against the American army in Georgia and Florida. Drawing taken from Thomas M'Kenney and James Hall. *From* History of the Indian Tribes of North America *(Philadelphia: Daniel Rice and James Clark, 1838–44).*

conclusion. Some historians date the beginnings of the wars—and there were three distinct wars— with the destruction of the so-called Negro Fort at Prospect Bluff on the Apalachicola River in 1816. Other historians point to the American attack on the Indian village of Fowltown, near present-day Bainbridge, Georgia, in November 1817. Still other historians date the beginning of the wars with the massacre of the unfortunate resupply mission of Lieutenant Richard W. Scott, who, along with forty soldiers, seven women and several children, was sent up the Apalachicola with supplies for an American fort located at the confluence of the Flint and Chattahoochee Rivers. General Edmund P. Gaines, the commander immediately in charge of Fort Scott and the surrounding area, quickly ordered his troops to be ready to march into Florida. Just as Gaines was getting ready to take the field, he was ordered by the new secretary of war, John C. Calhoun, to eliminate the pirates who had sailed to Amelia Island and taken control from the local Spanish commander.

With Gaines's departure, Andrew Jackson, who had replaced him, immediately moved his forces across the border into Spanish Florida. In order to avoid direct conflict with Spanish authorities, he was ordered to chastise the Seminoles for the attack on Lieutenant Scott's small group, notify Spanish officials of his orders and keep them abreast of his movements. Jackson was also instructed not to take any fortification or confront any Spanish force.

In a series of rapid movements and small engagements with Florida's Native Americans, Jackson's forces were able to drive the majority of them farther south away from the Georgia border. As he confronted the Indians, he encountered the British agents largely responsible for inciting them to attack the Spanish and American settlements. In a controversial decision, Jackson approved the execution of two of these agents, Alexander Arbuthnot and

Robert Ambrister, a move that signaled the United States would not tolerate British interference in Florida. Following up on evidence of the Spanish and their British allies supplying Indians in and around Pensacola with arms, Jackson marched on that town in May 1818 and demanded this action stop. Governor José Masot objected to such a demand, and the paper war began. Each man sent daily letters and demands to the other until Masot offered resistance by arms, whereupon Masot took his meager army to Fort Barrancas and Jackson drew up his six pieces of artillery. One shot was fired at the ancient fortification, and Masot surrendered, having honored his defense requirement. Almost every decision made by Jackson during this conflict was a source of controversy, and his assumption of power over the Spanish territory in West Florida was arrogant and unwarranted. However, he did accomplish his mission of punishing the Seminoles and making the Spanish well aware of their weaknesses in the face of an international seizure of their territory. It also set the stage for the Adams-Onis Treaty of 1819, which made Florida an American territory.

Throughout the 1820s, many of the rivers of northern Florida were explored and used to transport local produce to markets. Good lands on or near a navigable waterway were a natural magnet for settlement, and it is not surprising to find most of the newer settlements were located on or near such easy transportation routes. Settlers soon opened a number of local roads to the nearest navigable water course so as to ship their products to market. The army, even with limited funds and small numbers, also did its share of road building. In 1825, the army began construction of a road from Cantonment Brooke (Tampa) to Fort King (Ocala) and, in 1826, expanded it to Black Creek and the future site of Fort Heilman. Troops under Lieutenant Harvey Brown improved and extended the old King's Road south from St. Augustine to the Tomoka River in 1827–28. Congressional delegate Joseph Hernandez was easily persuaded by his constituents to get Congress to fund the army's first bridge across the St. Sebastian River. In 1823, Micanopy, the territory's oldest interior settlement, was connected to the St. Johns River at Palatka by a road that included eight bridges along the route. Roads were essential to reach the navigable waterways, and in 1829, the Territorial Council passed the Road Act, which required each county to establish a road commission and also gave the counties the complete authority to lay out and establish, change or discontinue roads within their boundaries. In addition, the Road Act gave the counties the right of eminent domain to condemn lands needed to construct the roads. Up to eight days of labor could be required of every

Isolated farms and plantations in Florida, usually located near a body of navigable water, were targets of Indian raids during the three Seminole Wars fought in the first half of the nineteenth century. *Courtesy of the Wynne Collection.*

able-bodied man—with the exception of teachers, physicians, postmasters, millers, pilots, preachers and ferrymen—to construct these roads.

The Road Act was promoted by the first civilian governor of Florida, William Pope Duval, who, on observing the lack of maintenance of the roads, pushed the tax, commutable to labor, to improve the transportation system and keep the roads passable. Some of this may have come because of the questionable condition of the famed Bellamy Road, which connected Middle Florida to St. Augustine and was infamous in its day for the tall stumps left in the middle of the road, which allegedly caused accidents and made travel by stage uncomfortable. In the 1820s and 1830s, roads were built to convey goods to places along the navigable rivers of the territory. Waterborne commerce was cheaper than crossing land on wagons pulled by draft animals.

Much of the early commerce of East Florida was carried by sailing vessels plying the waters of the St. Johns, Matanzas and Indian Rivers, as well as the smaller waterways connecting to them, especially the Tomoka River, Spruce Creek, Black Creek, Rice Creek and the Halifax River. The exploitation of these routes allowed this area to produce rice, indigo, naval stores and sugar in abundance, at least until the Second Seminole War (1835–42) brought things to a halt. Middle Florida, between the Suwannee and Apalachicola Rivers, also had a number of navigable rivers that reached into the heart of the Red Hills region. Most of the cotton and sugar produced in this area was transported by barges, flatboats and rafts down the Ochlockonee, Wakulla, St. Marks and some of the smaller rivers flowing into the Gulf of Mexico. Many of these latter rivers, like the Fenholloway, Econfina, Crystal River, Pithlachascotee, Weeki Wachee and Homosassa, were not accessible until after the Second Seminole War ended and many of the Native Americans were removed from Florida. West Florida had the Escambia, Blackwater, Yellow, Chipola, Choctawhatchee and Perdido Rivers available for deeper-draft craft like keelboats, schooners, sloops and some of the earliest steamboats.

Territorial Florida developed rapidly because of the existence of these numerous waterways. Unfortunately, some, like the Apalachicola, St. Johns and Suwannee Rivers, had substantial restrictions at their mouths, primarily sandbars, shoals and dangerous rock formations that had to be removed prior to more regular use. The Matanzas River at St. Augustine also suffered from constantly shifting sandbars and tidal action that inhibited the harbor's use.

On the Ocklawaha River, Fla.

Although from the post–Civil War era, this photograph illustrates the narrow width of many of the Florida rivers and the general construction of the small steamboats that plied them. *Courtesy of the Wynne Collection.*

The 1820s and 1830s also saw the beginnings of canal fever sweep across the nation, and Florida was not immune to it. In one of its very first issues, the Pensacola-based newspaper *The Floridian* presented the prospect of a canal between the Mississippi River and Pensacola. The editor claimed to be skeptical at first but was eventually convinced of its feasibility and the possibility of worldwide connections to markets by shipping through New Orleans. Dreams of rapid expansion and profits fueled the push for this canal and other, somewhat grandiose, projects such as a cross-Florida canal that would eliminate the lengthy and dangerous passage around the Keys. The dreams also expanded to include the possibility of a canal across Nicaragua to the Pacific Ocean, which would aid in the shipping of Florida products to markets hitherto thought unreachable.

In 1829, General Simon Bernard was hired by Congress to survey potential routes for a cross-Florida canal. Bernard's final report disappointed many when he recommended against constructing a canal along the routes he had surveyed because there was not "enough water at the top of the routes" to float the type and size of the barges or ships contemplated. While General Bernard was preparing his final report on the cross-Florida canal project, the governor and legislative council incorporated the Chipola Canal Company, which had the backing of some of the heavyweight politicians of West Florida, including Benjamin Chaires, Peter Gautier, Senator John Clark and William Hort. The major problem with this proposal was that it sought to raise the necessary funding via a lottery. The skepticism generated by this idea essentially killed the project, and it was never completed.

There were to be many subsequent surveys of possible canal routes in Florida. Some were privately funded, while others received initial funding from the territorial or federal governments. One such project, one of the shorter ones proposed, was the Pond Creek to Blackwater River canal. It was to be capitalized at a mere $10,000 but failed because of the Panic of 1837. Its sponsors did not have enough starter capital to construct the proposed canal. The survey was later used as the basis for the construction of the Arcadia Railroad over the same route, which was completed in 1838. The two largest canal incorporations in West Florida took place in 1835. The Chipola and St. Andrews Bay Company sought to connect the Chipola River with the bay. It was soon rivaled by the incorporation of the Lake Wimico and St. Joseph's Canal and Railroad Company. A plan for Lake Wimico and St. Joseph Canal was devised to link the Chipola and Apalachicola Rivers with St. Andrews Bay near St. Joseph, thereby diverting river traffic away from the port of Apalachicola to the new town of St. Joseph. In 1828, the

Lake Jackson Canal and Navigation Company came into existence. The object of this company was to connect the Ochlockonee River with Lake Jackson, then to the Wakulla River and then on to the port of St. Marks. The incorporation included permission to use Lakes Iamonia and Miccosukee and other ponds to connect to the Aucilla River. The 1831 incorporation of the Wacissa and Aucilla Navigation Company also involved canalization of these two rivers.

Some canal surveys were merely camouflage for other projects. For example, a federal survey for a canal between Fernandina and Cedar Keys was funded at the request of Senator David Levy Yulee in 1853. Although Yulee's survey was called a canal survey, it was really for what became the route for the Florida Railroad connecting Fernandina and Cedar Key. It had to be a canal survey because that is what Congress funded, not a railroad survey.

None of these proposed canals ever reached fruition during the territorial period. It was simply a matter of the financial weakness of the companies, the lack of qualified engineers and a small white labor force that was not willing to do the hard physical work required. Such skilled labor simply was not available in West Florida to successfully take on these projects, and slave labor was reserved for plantation work. Almost all of the main backers of these projects were planters who knew how to grow crops; they needed transportation to get them to market but had little practical experience in constructing canals or railroads.

David Levy Yulee, a railroad entrepreneur and a United States senator, constructed the first trans-Florida railroad from Fernandina to Cedar Keys. *Courtesy of the Wynne Collection.*

The arrival of steam-powered riverboats quickly replaced the planters' desire to build canals. Captain John Jenkins became the first steamboat captain to pilot his vessel up the strong current of the Apalachicola River in the fall of 1827. His paddle wheeler, *Fanny*, made the arduous trip upriver from Florida into Georgia to Columbus. Within three months, three other steamers joined the *Fanny*, and clearing the river became an ongoing concern. By 1835, a dozen other steamers were plying the waters of the Chattahoochee-Apalachicola system, hauling the products of southwestern Georgia and southeastern Alabama to Apalachicola. The former town of West Point changed its name in 1831 to reflect its specific location, Apalachicola. It grew rapidly and, by the time of the Civil War, had become the third-largest port on the Gulf of Mexico behind only New Orleans and Mobile. Improving the waterward approaches to the city and keeping the main channel clear of snags, shoals and fallen trees became full-time concerns.

Steamboats arrived on the St. Johns River with the docking of the ninety-foot side-wheeler *George Washington* in Jacksonville in May 1831. It had made the trip from Savannah in a mere thirty-four hours. Although Jacksonville was not then the bustling city it is today, it was on its way to becoming the main entry point to the St. Johns River and places farther south, upstream. The *George Washington* soon established a regular route from Savannah southward to Picolata, where passengers would debark for the relatively short trip by stage or foot into St. Augustine. The steamer *Florida* also began regular service from Savannah to Darien, St. Marys and then Jacksonville before continuing to Picolata in 1834.

The traffic pattern along the St. Johns dramatically changed with the outbreak of the Second Seminole War (1835–42). Many states and communities contributed volunteers to fight, and almost all of them arrived by steamboats or sailing ships. Over forty steamers were contracted with to supply and carry the army into the field. As Edward Mueller noted, "Transportation by water played a key role….Because of the lack of roads, they served as logical and logistical answers to military needs. Army facilities located on or near navigable waters, like the St. Johns River and its tributaries, could be supplied by steamboats." Most of the steamboats operating in the St. Johns were strictly for military purposes. At this point in time, there was little demand for civilian use of these valuable craft.

Immediately after the destruction of Major Francis Dade's command near modern Bushnell in December 1835, the frontier was in turmoil and confusion. Dade's command constituted nearly one-fifth of the army's available forces, and its elimination created a real problem for the remaining military, which feared the Seminoles would make a concerted effort to destroy the American outpost at Tampa Bay. However, ships from the U.S. Navy arrived with marine reinforcements, soon followed by three revenue cutters and another force from Louisiana. The threat was averted.

Little was known about the interior lands below Tampa Bay or the Gulf Coast. This was remedied somewhat when Captain M.P. Mix of the *Concord* sailed northward and then returned, mapping as he went. Mix's maps were

Billy Bowlegs, also known as Holata Micco, was an important leader of the Seminoles in Florida during the Second Seminole and Third Seminole Wars, when he led the Seminoles' last major resistance against the U.S. government. *Courtesy of the Wynne Collection.*

good enough to keep most of the larger ships out of danger and gave an idea as to the number of inlets and passes that were available to use. Mix's survey had been preceded in 1830–31 by a timber survey along the western coast of Florida for live oak and cedar by Colonel Sam Reid. Under his command, navy yawls and Whitehalls went up almost every river and navigable stream along the western coast. The purpose was to reserve large parcels of land containing these useful trees for naval purposes.

Covering the area southward from Tampa Bay was a bit more dangerous than the 1830–31 timber surveys since it was mostly done by the army following the outbreak of the war. Lieutenant John T. McLaughlin led boats from the Mosquito Fleet to the southern end of the peninsula and mapped the numerous islands and mangrove forests at the edge of the Everglades. McLaughlin also led his men into the Everglades. As John Mahon noted, "In a flotilla of dugouts, John T. McLaughlin led an expedition from December 1840 to mid-January 1841, across the entire peninsula from east to west. His was the first party of white men ever to cross the full width of the Everglades." McLaughlin's explorations were followed a year later by those of Commodore John Rodgers, who also took dugouts across part of the Everglades and sailed across Lake Okeechobee and up Fisheating Creek to the Indian mounds at Venus.

Steamboating on the St. Johns and other Florida rivers declined during the Seminole War but picked up rapidly after it ended. Many of the steamers, like the *Santee* and the *William Gaston*, became the nucleus of a corps of steamers serving the flourishing trade in lumber, cotton and cane syrup. By 1850, several new towns had developed along the St. Johns River, and places like Palatka and Picolata, now connected to St. Augustine by a rudimentary railroad, began to grow. The lumber industry contributed to the growth of Middleburg on Black Creek, and on Lake Monroe the town of Enterprise became an important shipping point and tourist destination. Jacksonville's growth was based on the lumber trade, and in 1850, the first circular sawmill began operation there. Florida's growing population also demanded mail service, and much of the mail was carried by steamers on Florida's rivers. Navigational aids, lighthouses and houses of refuge began to appear along the coasts and rivers, making travel by ships and boats safer. The improvements for water travel continued even after Florida was admitted to the Union on March 3, 1845.

3

KEY WEST, ISLAND AT THE CROSSROADS

Key West, the southernmost port in the United States, occupies a strategic position where the Gulf of Mexico, the Atlantic Ocean and the Florida Straits come together as main shipping lanes to Central and South America, as well as Mexico and the Gulf states. A small and isolated island barely four square miles in area, Key West did not generate any interest from Spain or Great Britain during their periods of ownership. From the time of its discovery by Ponce de Leon in 1513 until the beginning of the American territorial period in 1821, the island had no permanent structures and its few residents were either shipwrecked sailors, salvors of wrecked ships, fishermen or pirates seeking momentary shelter in its deep natural harbor. So little interest in the island was manifested by the Spanish or the British that the island was deeded to a private owner, Juan Pablo Salas, in 1815. Salas, who had no interest in developing the island, subsequently sold it (twice) to American businessmen, first to John Geddes and later to John W. Simington. After much contentious litigation, Simington managed to gain a clear title to the island.

Although Simington quickly subdivided the island into quarter portions and sold three of them to friends, it was the arrival of the U.S. Navy in 1822 that brought it to the attention of Americans. They were impressed by the deep-water anchorage, which ranged from twenty-two to thirty-six feet, and the numerous small islands nearby that offered some protection from hurricanes and violent storms. The port seemed to fit all the requirements for conducting naval operations in the southern Atlantic, the Gulf and the

Caribbean. The only drawback was the lack of a land connection, which meant that all supplies, including fresh water, would have to be brought in by ships. Nevertheless, by 1823 the island was under the control of Commodore David Porter, the commander of the West Indies Anti-Pirate Squadron, who ruled as a virtual dictator.

From the deep-water harbor, navy ships could closely monitor and control the many ships that used the nearby waters. Commodore Porter recognized the importance of establishing a naval base at Key West when, in November 1823, he wrote, "The fixing an establishment at Thompson's Island (Key West) for rendezvous and supplies has had a most happy effect in attaining the object [we] had in view. Its vicinity to Havana, placed as it were, in the thoroughfare of vessels sailing through the gulf, making it, in many points of view, an object of great importance to the United States." Commodore John Rodgers, president of the Board of Navy Commissioners, concurred with Porter's assessment:

> *Nature had made it the advance post from which to watch and guard our commerce passing to and from the Mississippi, while at the same time, its peculiar situation, and the excellence of its harbor, point it out as the most certain key to the commerce of Havana, to that of the whole Gulf of Mexico, and to the returning trade of Jamaica; and I venture to predict, that the first important naval contest in which this country shall be engaged will be in the neighborhood of this very island.*

Rodgers's comments were a prescient forecast of the future. Just thirty-eight years later, Key West and its naval base played a key role as the linchpin in the Union's control of the Florida coasts. In 1898, its importance was again highlighted when American ships used it as a base for operations against the Spanish possessions in the Caribbean during the Spanish-American War. In World War I and World War II, the Key West base served as a strategic element in American efforts to control German submarines preying on shipping in the Atlantic and Gulf. For two hundred years, Key West has been a critical base of operations for the American military in the Gulf of Mexico, the Florida Straits and the Atlantic. Today, its proximity to Cuba, a bare ninety miles away from the communist regime created by the Castro brothers, makes it the ideal base for monitoring events in that island nation, as evidenced by the role Key West played in the 1961 Cuban Missile Crisis.

The arrival of the U.S. Navy to the island of Key West brought about an immediate and lasting transformation. No longer was it just a largely deserted island sleeping in the warm tropical sunshine and only occasionally visited by fishermen or pirates, but it now took on additional importance as the nation's major military base protecting its Latin and South American interests. So important had Key West become that immediately after Florida was granted statehood in 1845, the army began construction of a fort, Fort Zachary Taylor, to protect the United States' southern border. Despite momentary setbacks caused by outbreaks of "yellow jack" (malaria) and frequent shortages of building materials, construction continued throughout the 1850s and into the 1860s.

A year later, the federal government began work on Fort Thomas Jefferson in the Dry Tortugas, a chain of eleven small islands located some seventy miles west of Key West. Despite having been declared uninhabitable and of little military value by Commodore Porter when he inspected them in late 1824 and early 1825—although he did recommend the construction of a lighthouse to guide ships around the islands—a later survey party under the leadership of Joseph Tattnall III found many advantages to the militarization of the Tortugas. Tattnall's evaluation of the importance of the small islands to national security found ready support from the army's best

Key West quickly became a major base for the American navy following the acquisition of the port in 1821–22, and Commodore David Porter, the commanding officer of the West Indies Squadron, recommended the construction of a fort to protect it. Fort Zachary Taylor met that need. *Courtesy of the Wynne Collection.*

engineer, Robert E. Lee, and from navy captain John G. Barnard, who made a detailed survey of the islands' potential in 1844. In 1845, the Dry Tortugas were declared a military reservation, and plans were drawn for a massive fort to be built on Garden Key. Construction began in 1846 and continued until the early 1870s.

The American occupation of the Florida Keys was always in recognition of its military potential, as evidenced by the report of a naval committee chaired by Captain, later Admiral, Samuel Francis DuPont in early 1861. Charged with the mission of determining a strategy that would ensure federal control of the coastlines of Confederate states, the DuPont Commission noted, "At Key West are stores of coal, water, and munitions of war…[and] Fort Jefferson, at the Tortugas, and Fort Taylor, at Key West, with certain supplementary works, will easily hold this part of the coast against any but a first-rate naval power." The commission's recommendations for additional subsidiary fortifications were quickly answered by the construction of the East and West Martellos, small brick emplacements that served as outlying artillery batteries.

Not all residents of Key West depended on the military for their livelihoods, and the small city developed a diverse and viable economy. Within the first two decades following the American occupation of Key West, it quickly became the major entrepôt for Florida and the other southern states that bordered the Gulf of Mexico. Just as the American navy made use of the deep harbors at Key West and Fort Jefferson, so, too, did the small coastal schooners that plied the waters from northern Florida ports like Apalachicola, St. Marks and Bayport. Laden with cotton and tobacco destined for the lucrative markets of Europe, these smaller ships used Key West as a transfer point where goods would be transferred to larger oceangoing vessels. In exchange, cargoes of manufactured and luxury items arrived regularly from Europe and were offloaded into warehouses and stored until the same schooners that brought agricultural products to the port could be reloaded and make their way north to the small bays, rivers and ports along the coast. With few inland roads and no railroads until the 1860s in the state, the ports, usually located at the mouths of rivers and large creeks, became points of distribution for Florida's thriving agrarian economy. As a result, warehouse storage space was always at a premium in Key West, and the city prospered.

Key West grew rapidly. With the American acquisition of the Keys in 1821 and the navy's decision to make use of the deep-water harbor, coupled with the bustling civilian trade, the city experienced a continuous pattern of population growth during the years immediately following. As a southern city, slavery was common in Key West, and the population of enslaved persons grew as rapidly as the white population. So, too, did the number of free African Americans, who were employed in various roles in the city. Throughout the territorial period and until the Civil War, Key West remained southern in its outlook and politics, a situation that would present problems for federal authorities with the start of the Civil War in 1861.

Evidence of the importance of Key West as a transit point for civilian shipping can be found by the establishment of a customhouse in the city immediately after the United States took control. According to Jefferson B. Browne, who published a history of the island in 1912, the annual tax revenues collected by customs officials during the period 1828 to 1832 averaged $45,000 per year, an amount equal to roughly $1.41 million today. Annual customs revenues continued to rise throughout the antebellum period. The customs revenues in Key West were so great that in 1888, the federal government spent the enormous sum of $107,955 on the construction of a new, all-brick customhouse.

Because of the volume of shipping through the port of Key West and the potential for conflict about issues relating to the process, the need quickly arose for some sort of court to decide matters in dispute. In 1828, Key West was designated as an official "port of entry" and an admiralty court was created. According to the Admiralty Records for Key West, maintained by the National Archives, the scope of authority for an admiralty court is broad and deals with "prize, ransom, salvage cases, ownership, maritime contracts, and torts. Maritime contracts relate to charter, passenger transportation, baggage, loading and unloading, salvage, seaman's wages, and the care of injured seamen. Maritime torts relate to collisions, loss, or damage of cargo, and claims of personal injury."

The location of such a court in the city was important because the Federal Wrecking Act of 1825 specified that all property recovered in American waters be taken to the nearest admiralty court. The nearest admiralty courts were in St. Augustine or Pensacola, some five hundred miles distant, a journey that could take weeks and was inconvenient and expensive. Because captured blockade runners were sent to Key West during the Civil War, the admiralty court took on additional importance, since the value of the captured ship and cargo was awarded to the men and officers of the capturing ship or ships.

"Wrecking," or salvaging wrecked ships, was a major industry for some Key West residents, who carefully monitored the movement of ships through the Keys. Hidden reefs and banks, coupled with hurricanes and ocean storms, always made such journeys perilous. Despite the installation of "lights, buoys, and beacons…under the supervision of the United States government" as required by the Congressional Act of May 23, 1828, reducing the number of hazards for ships, accidents still happened. It was not until the adaptation of steam power to ships and the decline in the number of sailing ships in the mid-1850s that the number of wrecks decreased. Steam power provided ships with the ability to sail against prevailing winds and to withstand hurricanes, although even some steamships floundered and wrecked.

Indeed, some critics of the wrecking industry went so far as to accuse the Key West wreckers of deliberately luring ships onto the reefs and banks by displaying false lights or beacons or by rearranging those put in place by the government. In 1942, Cecil B. DeMille chose to emphasize this sordid side of the wrecking business in his film *Reap the Wild Wind*. In July 1823, the Legislative Council of the Territory of Florida enacted a salvage law that was aimed at bringing order to the wrecking business and codifying how salvage operations should be conducted. This law was the first effort by an American governmental institution to regulate the salvage industry. The Florida act was soon followed by the passage of a federal statute, the Federal Wrecking Act, in 1825, which imposed tighter restrictions on salvage operations.

Despite the protestations of residents and government officials that the wrecking profession was an honorable one, largely free of fraud or criminality, the public perception of wreckers as unscrupulous and dishonest persisted. As Charles Walker wrote in an 1838 letter to his aunt and uncle Lydia and Timothy Walker in New Hampshire, "The general opinion entertained of Key West is, that it is a sickly & very immoral place, the former abode of pirates & the present residence of wreckers, who are but little better." Walker denied such allegations and declared that Key West "is more moral than any other [place] of its size that I can recollect." Dr. Benjamin B. Strobel, a Charleston physician who arrived in Key West in 1829, also commented on the character of the city's inhabitants in an article published in the *Charleston Courier* on May 13, 1837: "I come now to speak of the inhabitants of Key West. I am unwilling to do them injustice. Many are generous and liberal, to the sick, the stranger, and unfortunate, kind and benevolent. It cannot, however, be denied that there is a great want of moral feeling in the community."

In 1942, Cecil B. DeMille adapted Thelma Strabel's best-selling novel *Reap the Wild Wind* into a hit movie. It portrays the story of Key West wreckers and cutthroat salvagers who went from salvaging the wrecks of transatlantic cargo ships to causing them. *Courtesy of the Wynne Collection.*

Walker, an aspiring lawyer, noted that the entire population of Key West was tied to wrecking directly or indirectly. His observation was echoed by Strobel, who wrote, "The principal revenue of this place [Key West] must be derived, for the present at least, from the Florida Reef." The amount of salvaged goods and ships brought to Key West rose considerably throughout the 1830s and 1840s, and the auxiliary enterprises associated with storing and disposing of the rescued merchandise grew accordingly. Warehouses, repair yards, chandleries and auction houses dominated the local economy. Wreckers, whose incomes were based on a percentage of the appraised value of salvaged cargoes, usually 10 percent plus reimbursement for expenses, generously spent their money on purchasing the very goods they had salvaged. Three major auction houses controlled most of the sales of the cargoes. One auctioneer is reported to have made more than $10,000 in commissions in a single year, which in 2022 dollars is more than $300,000.

The amount of money returned to citizens of Key West through salvage awards and expense payments was a staggering $1,631,845 in 1850 dollars, a sum that translates into a whopping $61,984,167.85 in today's dollars or roughly $24,793 for each of the city's 2,500 residents for the six-year period or $4,132 per year. The influx of so much wealth in such a small community made Key West one of the wealthiest cities in the United States per capita by the 1840s, a designation it maintained until the beginning of the Civil War in 1861.

Although all the city's residents were affected by wrecking or shipping in some way, not everyone shared in the wealth of the wreckers, auctioneers or their families. Enterprising individuals who were not part of the maritime industry soon sought other ways in which to capitalize on the wealth of the city. Among the first indigenous enterprises to develop on the island was the collection and manufacture of salt. There was a universal demand for salt and in great quantities. Used for the preservation of meats of all kinds—beef, pork and mutton—salt was also essential for the preservation of fish caught in nearby waters, to allow them to be shipped to northern markets. In addition, salt was a commonly used seasoning in most kitchens. Some small quantities had been collected from small natural salt ponds on the island, but none of the early residents possessed sufficient capital thought to be necessary to embark on a large-scale production of salt until Richard Fitzpatrick leased tidal flood lands on the southeastern end of the island in 1830. Using a crude system of "pans" excavated from coral rock formations, he created a series of floodgates that would allow him to flood the pans with salt water, which was then allowed to evaporate. By repeating this process several times a year, a thin crust of salt was formed on the bottom of the pans. This crust was harvested, broken into smaller crystals, bagged and sent to markets throughout the world. The beauty of this kind of operation was that it required little initial investment of cash since no machinery was necessary, and the price for the finished product was always stable and high. In 1830, a bushel of salt, which weighed approximately fifty pounds, sold for $2.25. In 2022 dollars, the value would be $74.57 a bushel or $1.49 a pound. A local newspaper editor, enthralled by the simplicity of the production process and the high prices of the marketplace, predicted that soon production would require more than five hundred ships to transport the salt to market.

Despite its early promise, salt production on Key West failed to live up to the expectations of investors. While the actual cost of production remained low, international competition and the vagaries of the island's tropical weather proved devastating. Some years, annual rains came early and diluted the salt in the evaporation pans; other years, hurricanes wiped out an entire year's work; and sometimes political events, such as the Civil War, curtailed production. Nevertheless, salt production continued to attract the hopeful until around 1871, when the last salt operation closed.

Among the non-wrecker businesses to develop in Key West was sponging, which required little investment and, after a fitful start, proved to be a profitable enterprise. Prior to 1849, sponges used by Americans were shipped from the Mediterranean or from Africa, but a test shipment of Key West sponges to New York proved that they were cheaper and more desirable than foreign ones. A new industry was born. The shallow banks around the Keys were ideal for growing high-quality sponges, and the crystal-clear water allowed spongers to use small boats from which sponges could be harvested using a simple tool called the hook, a three- or four-pronged rake, curved to allow the sponger to pry a sponge loose and bring it to the surface. No machinery or complicated technology was needed for the industry. An estimated 150 small boats were used in sponging operations, and eventually the sale of sponges to northern markets added an additional $750,000 annually to the island's economy.

As early as 1831, the cigar industry was important to Key West. In that year, William H. Wall established a factory that employed some fifty workers. Using tobacco imported from Cuba, the cigars produced in Key West were popular in New York and other northern cities. Although a small operation, the establishment of the Wall factory encouraged others to follow his example, and within ten years several more small factories had opened in the city. Despite the popularity of Key West cigars, the industry remained small because of the irregular schedules of ships to take the factories' output to northern markets. Several other minor industries developed in Key West during the antebellum period. Turtling, a canning factory, shrimping, growing Key limes and pineapples and fishing claimed a small portion of the local economy but remained secondary to enterprises directly tied to the larger maritime pursuits.

The Key West social life also thrived during the mid-1800s. Charles Walker, the recent arrival from New Hampshire, described the evolving social scene in an 1838 letter:

> *The society of the place is, of course, small, but there are many families from the Atlantic States now our residents, that would be very desirable acquisitions were they to return to the places of their nativity. In their dinner and evening parties, there is the same taste & I am sorry to add the same luxury & display that you find in large cities. More good books, reviews & late publications are found here than you have the most distant idea of. Indeed we require them, for we have not the different ways to pass our time that those have who can ride and journey at pleasure.*

Although the opportunities for engaging in a variety of activities might have been limited in Key West, Walker found things to do to fill his leisure hours. There were opportunities for social interaction between the sexes on the island, and Walker described an active social life:

> *About once a week in the winter we have a party in the evening & the ladies dress, dance and waltz with great skill & taste, especially the descendants of the Spaniards. We can easily form three cotillions, or two Spanish dances, & so passionately fond of this amusement are the ladies, & I suppose I may add gentlemen, that the music ceases not near the first grey of the morning.*

James C. Hoyt, an agent for the New York Board of Underwriters, gave a further description of Key West in 1850 in a report to his employers in that city. The island, he wrote, "has two schools, and Episcopal, Roman Catholic, Methodist, and Baptist congregations and churches each having its own clergyman. There is certainly a great improvement going on in the moral and social condition of the inhabitants, and they will bear comparison in these respects with any marine town in our country of its size."

From its obscure and neglected status as a part of Spanish Florida, Key West emerged as a vital port following its cession to the United States in 1821. Within the short span of four decades, it had become both one of the wealthiest cities in the nation and among the largest in Florida. Its location at the tip of the Florida Keys ensured it played a dominant role in American foreign policy and military strategy for the next two hundred years. As a maritime hub, it served both civilian and military needs—and prospered because of both.

4

ANTEBELLUM FLORIDA

PRELUDE TO THE CIVIL WAR

*J*ust fifteen years after Florida became a state, Floridians took the extreme step of joining the newly formed Confederate States of America. Although it was a step opposed by some Floridians, the decision to secede reflected the reality that Florida was very much a southern slave state. Slaveholders operated plantations, large and small, which produced approximately 90 percent of the state's wealth. This wealth, concentrated in ten or twelve counties along the northern rim and center of Florida, secured control of the state's political system for slave owners, many of whom had close and direct family ties with the planter families in other southern states. These familial ties, coupled with similar economic interests and the relative newness of the state's slave-based economy, produced a Florida that has been described as the "most southern of the southern states." The state's commitment to its "southernness" was no more evident than in its decision to follow South Carolina and Mississippi into the uncharted seas of southern independence.

According to the census of 1860, Florida's population totaled 140,424 persons. Of these, 77,747 were white, 932 were free Black people and 61,745 were enslaved. The upper half of the peninsula was suitable for the cultivation of two cash crops traditionally grown in the plantation South, tobacco and cotton, and the newly created plantations of the region concentrated on them. When these scions of planters arrived, they brought with them slaves from other states and gradually increased their numbers through the purchase of new ones. In addition, the state's slave population grew because of natural reproduction. Generally, individuals who owned

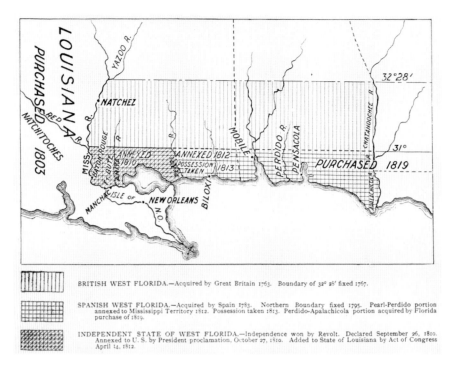

BRITISH WEST FLORIDA.—Acquired by Great Britain 1763. Boundary of 32° 28' fixed 1767.

SPANISH WEST FLORIDA.—Acquired by Spain 1783. Northern Boundary fixed 1795. Pearl-Perdido portion annexed to Mississippi Territory 1812. Possession taken 1813. Perdido-Apalachicola portion acquired by Florida purchase of 1819.

INDEPENDENT STATE OF WEST FLORIDA.—Independence won by Revolt. Declared September 26, 1810. Annexed to U. S. by President proclamation, October 27, 1810. Added to State of Louisiana by Act of Congress April 14, 1812.

Planters in the southern states of Louisiana, Mississippi, Alabama and Georgia used Pensacola as a major shipping point for their crops of cotton and tobacco bound for European markets. *Map from Henry E. Chambers, 1860–1929—West Florida and Its Relation to the Historical Cartography of the United States (Baltimore, MD: Johns Hopkins Press, 1898).*

twenty or more slaves were classified as planters, while those engaged in agriculture with fewer slaves were regarded as "large farmers." Despite this arbitrary system of classification, the interests of planters and large farmers were bound together.

Like other southern states, Florida during the antebellum period was a highly stratified society. Despite constituting less than 5 percent of Florida's population, planters dominated the social and political life of the state, which, when coupled with their economic dominance, allowed them to control affairs in the state. Professional persons—doctors, lawyers, surveyors and others—were closely tied to the planter elite and tended to adopt their views. Some of these professionals entered the planter ranks through marriage or by accumulating enough wealth to purchase their own plantations. Beneath the planters and professional classes were the shopkeepers, artisans, factors and skilled craftsmen whose livelihoods depended on maintaining good relations with the monied classes and who tended to defer to them in politics and other matters. Some were also slaveholders, owning one or two slaves.

The lowest social and economic class for Florida whites was made up of small farmers and stockmen. Their operations tended to be small and focused on raising foodstuffs or livestock. Most of these small farms and ranches were in the most isolated areas of the state, usually on lands considered unfit for cotton or tobacco cultivation. Like the townspeople, some of these individuals were slave owners, enslaving one or two laborers who worked alongside them. For example, the 1860 census noted that in Brevard County, one of the southernmost occupied counties on the Florida mainland, there were 20 slaves and 1 free Black male living among a white population of 224. Most of these were enslaved by Douglass Dummett, who was engaged in growing citrus on the north end of Merritt Island. John Carroll Houston, who operated a small plantation in Arlington, later renamed Eau Gallie, in Brevard County also held slaves, although how many is unknown. While most of the state's white population were not slave owners, they aspired to be simply because slave ownership usually equated to social and economic success.

Given the geography of antebellum Florida, most towns and cities were located adjacent to a body of water—a river, the Gulf of Mexico or the

Slaveholding planters, scions of planters' families in southern states, dominated the economic, political and social life of territorial Florida, and they sought to replicate the privileged lifestyle they had enjoyed before coming to Florida. *Courtesy of the Wynne Collection.*

Atlantic Ocean—because the road system in the state was underdeveloped and water routes provided the easiest and fastest way to transport agricultural products to market and to import essential supplies and luxury items. In the more highly developed northern Panhandle, cities and towns were located within one hundred miles of the Gulf Coast. Small ports, like Apalachicola and St. Marks, handled the tobacco and cotton crops from nearby plantations, loading the cargoes on small clipper ships bound for Key West, Pensacola, Mobile or some other port where they could be transferred to larger oceangoing vessels. Flat-bottomed barges laden with bales of cotton and tobacco navigated the small rivers that fed into the Gulf.

Pensacola, located at the extreme western edge of Florida, served as a collection point and a major shipping terminal for plantation crops from lower Alabama and the Panhandle. In addition, Pensacola was the transshipment port for timber from Okaloosa and Santa Rosa Counties. These two counties supplied 53 percent of the yellow pine timber harvested in the state, and the Blackwater River, which emptied into Pensacola Bay, provided an excellent way to transport heavy cargoes of timber. Two additional rivers, the Perdido and the Escambia, emptied into Pensacola Bay, and they, too, served as transportation routes to the port.

Tallahassee, located in the heart of the Panhandle's plantation region, was only twenty miles from the small port of St. Marks at Apalachee Bay. As the plantation economy grew, St. Marks's importance as a port grew. Although a short distance from Tallahassee, the roads between the two towns were difficult to navigate, and in 1836, a wooden-railed, horse-and-mule-powered railroad was built to haul cotton from South Georgia and Panhandle plantations. Port Leon, Magnolia and St. Marks prospered for a few years until an 1843 hurricane obliterated Port Leon and seriously damaged Magnolia. Completed in 1837, the Tallahassee–St. Marks Railroad was a success. In 1837, an estimated thirty thousand bales of cotton moved over the railroad and out to markets in Europe. In 1856, the wooden rails and animal-drawn cars were replaced with steel rails and steam engines.

Despite possessing a large and deep bay, protected by outlying barrier islands, Cedar Keys was not considered an important port during the antebellum period. Accessible only by water, the island was isolated. A lighthouse was located on Seahorse Key, an adjacent island, to guide ships along the coast. Cedar Keys was situated an equidistance between the Sewanee River to the northwest and the Crystal River to the southeast, both minor rivers with little traffic. The arrival of the cross-Florida railroad in

The Grove, the plantation home of two-term territorial governor Richard Keith Call, was located in the area at the heart of modern-day Tallahassee, Florida's capital. *Courtesy of Florida Memory*.

Tallahassee, the capital of Florida, was a small town with dirt streets and unimpressive wooden buildings during the territorial period. As the cotton plantations developed in Florida, the town grew accordingly and soon rivaled the capitals of other older southern states. *Courtesy of Florida Memory*.

1860 offered the possibility that the city's fortunes would grow rapidly, a possibility that did not become a reality until the 1870s.

Tampa Bay and Charlotte Harbor were also deep-water harbors but were not used very much. The sparse population on the southwest coast of the peninsula did not produce enough agricultural products to merit a high volume of shipping. The fishing industry dominated Charlotte Harbor and the surrounding area, while both ports did export a significant number of beeves each year. Still, compared to more active ports like St. Marks and Pensacola, these ports were not considered important points in the water transportation of Florida. However, they provided easy access to the Caloosahatchee, Peace, Manatee and Hillsborough Rivers, which led to the interior of the peninsula.

Key West, located at the end of the Florida Keys, continued its reign as the most important transshipment port in Florida, although the completion of David Levy Yulee's Florida Railroad from Fernandina to Cedar Key threatened its dominance. On the Atlantic Coast, Fernandina, located at the mouth of the St. Marys River, was considered the best deep-water port. The St. Marys was the southern border of Georgia and the northern border of Florida. Its deep-water harbor was ideal to handle transoceanic ships, and the products of northeastern Florida and southeastern Georgia plantations, as well as naval stores and lumber from South Georgia forests, found their way there.

Twenty miles south of Fernandina was the port of Jacksonville. It was founded in 1822 near the site of the old cow ford across the broad St. Johns River, and the census of 1850 counted a population of 1,145 residents, but that had increased significantly by 1860. Like other Florida ports at the time, Jacksonville's economy depended heavily on the export of cotton, lumber and foodstuffs to national and international markets. In return, it received cargoes of manufactured goods from the same markets and distributed these goods to towns and villages along the river. Unlike other rivers in the state, the St. Johns flowed northward from the heart of the peninsula for a distance of some 310 miles.

St. Augustine is the oldest city in Florida and was a busy port during the antebellum period. However, the depth of the Matanzas River and the fact that the Matanzas was an estuary with water levels that rose and fell with the changing tides made it less than desirable as a commercial port. Between St. Augustine and the Keys, only New Smyrna operated as an active port. Established during the British period of control, New Smyrna provided an outlet for the sugar plantations that were located there. The Tomoka River, which ran from the coast and connected to the St. Johns River, provided access to the interior of the state. Although small, New Smyrna was a port with great potential as the state's population increased. Ponce Inlet north of New Smyrna had no port, but it connected to the Mosquito Lagoon, where the multitude of channels and islands offered shelter and safety for the small coastal schooners that plied the coast.

Still farther south, the Indian River Lagoon stretched 156 miles from Mosquito Inlet to present-day Jupiter. A shallow nontidal basin protected by barrier islands, the lack of navigable inlets prevented its use as a major water transportation route, although the few residents along its shores used flat-bottomed barges and small boats to traverse its length and harvest its bounty of fish, oysters, turtles and other items. The absence of roads into the interior along its shores further reduced its importance. By virtue of the absence of inlets into the lagoon and its shallowness, only small sailboats and skiffs could operate in it. Despite its limitations, the lagoon was a vital waterway used by the small population in the region. Its proximity to the St. Johns River, as close as five miles in some areas, provided an entrée into the interior regions of Florida. Along the extreme southern Atlantic Coast, several small bays and rivers existed, but the absence of a significant population lessened their importance. The same could be said about Biscayne Bay and the Miami River.

At the beginning of the Civil War in April 1861, southern states accounted for 70 percent of the American export economy, and of this, cotton exports made up roughly 75 percent. So dominant was cotton in the overall economy that David Christy published a book titled *Cotton Is King* in 1855. It extolled the virtues of the cash crop and promoted the growth of the institution of slavery despite Christy's recognition of the movement toward mechanization in agriculture. "King Cotton" became the slogan of choice for the South.

European textile mills depended almost entirely on southern cotton, while the majority of consumer and luxury items used in southern states came from Europe. Despite the slowly increasing number of textile mills in northern states, the reality was that the economies of the states that made up the newly formed Confederacy were more closely tied to European countries than they were to states in the North. Although some factories were built in the larger towns and cities of the South, northern states could claim five times more factories and more than ten times the number of skilled factory workers. Those southern factories that did exist were generally geared toward manufacturing light industrial goods while northern factories focused on iron foundries and heavy industries in addition to textile mills producing cotton and woolen goods. Although the South possessed considerable deposits of iron and coal, little had been done to use or exploit them. The emphasis on growing cotton as a cash crop took precedence.

While the elite planter class in Florida grew wealthy from cotton and tobacco production, little attention had been paid to the development of the basic infrastructure needed to sustain an industrial economy. Southerners believed that cotton was critical to European factories and made up such a high percentage of American exports that the states that produced this staple were vital to the continued progress of the United States. To interfere with its cultivation, they argued, would lead to the collapse of the entire American economy.

During the antebellum period, the southern states felt threatened by two major issues supported by northern politicians and businessmen. The first was the issue of protective tariffs and the effect such tariffs would have on the South. Because the major markets for American cotton were in England and France and because southerners used the factor system of banking whereby cotton was sold abroad through an agent who used a significant amount of the proceeds to purchase European goods, the bulk of southern wealth went to overseas manufacturers and merchants. Northern political leaders argued that imposing a protective tariff was necessary to raise the price of such goods above the price of similar domestically produced products, thereby stimulating American manufacturing and making it competitive with the older, more established foreign factories. The unique sell/buy arrangement of the factor system meant the imposition of protective tariffs would immediately decrease their wealth and force them to pay a tax to support northern industries.

The first major crisis over protective tariffs occurred in 1832 when South Carolina called for a convention to declare the federal tariffs of 1828 and 1832 unconstitutional and to nullify their enforcement within the boundaries of that state. Continued enforcement of the tariffs against the expressed wishes of the state could lead to the withdrawal of South Carolina from the Union. This theory of secession was part and parcel of the concept of state rights, wherein the authority of any state took precedence over that of the federal government within state boundaries. Vice President John C. Calhoun, the leading proponent of the doctrine of nullification and secession, led the movement and resigned his office to run for the U.S. Senate where he could more effectively defend these theories in open debate.

President Andrew Jackson rejected South Carolina's argument and called on Congress to pass the Force Bill, which would allow him to increase the army to 100,000 soldiers. "I intend to invade South Carolina," Jackson is reputed to have remarked to a southern congressman, "and hang every damned man there, beginning with the vice-president!" Jackson's dislike of Calhoun stemmed from an attempt by Calhoun to have Jackson censured after he invaded Florida in 1817 and from the actions of Calhoun and his wife in the notorious Peggy Eaton scandal.

The issue of protective tariffs continued to be a bone of contention between the North and the South. Throughout the South, political leaders railed against even moderate tariffs, while northern leaders and businessmen argued that such tariffs were essential to the continued development of the industrial capacity of the United States. Matters came to a head again in 1850 when southern states convened in Nashville to protest against the passage of another protective tariff and to argue that if Congress did not repeal the tariff or replace it with a more moderate one, the cotton-producing states would be left with no alternative but to secede from the Union. Despite the growing popularity of the theory of secession—that the Union was a voluntary association of states and any state that was unhappy with the actions of the federal government could leave the Union—cooler heads prevailed, and a compromise was reached.

Protective tariffs were not the only issues that riled southerners during the antebellum period. The antislavery movement, which had its nexus in the North, was slowly gaining more adherents and sympathizers. Abolition became a curse word firmly entrenched in the vernacular of the South, and abolitionists were regarded as the spawn of the devil intent on destroying the society based on slavery and cotton production. Northern ministers and reformers such as William Lloyd Garrison, Theodore Weld and Henry Ward Beecher railed against slavery, while newspapers of the region gave free publicity to the exploits of those who escaped slavery like Henry "Box" Brown, Sojourner Truth, Frederick Douglass and Harriet Tubman. The abolitionists attracted some followers in the South, most notably the Grimké sisters of Virginia.

In March 1807, Congress passed An Act Prohibiting the Importation of Slaves, which became effective on January 1, 1808, and was the product of an earlier agreement between northern and southern states. However, as the cotton economy grew over the next several decades, the prohibition on slavery became more onerous to southern planters. Although it did restrict the numbers of slaves brought into the United States and limited available laborers for plantations, it also had the effect of making slaves more valuable and, as a result, stimulated the growth of an illicit slave trade. As the value of individual slaves increased, so, too, did the resistance of planters to any attack on the institution.

Despite the growing strength of the abolitionist movement in the United States and abroad, southerners maintained their ability to thwart efforts to do away with slavery. Their power rested on their control of the federal political system. Southern states, through the constitutionally guaranteed representation in the Electoral College and the Senate, could block any effort to abolish slavery and control presidential elections during the antebellum period. A compromise in the Constitution granted southern states the right to count slaves as three-fifths of a person in population counts, a measure that allowed an increased southern presence in the House of Representatives. In addition, southerners also tended to control the makeup of the Supreme Court, which usually followed a strict construction ideology.

At the heart of the South's ability to withstand northern efforts to limit or abolish slavery was the Missouri Compromise of 1820, a measure that declared that the American West would be arbitrarily divided into slaveholding and slave-free sections along a line of 36° 30′ and that new slaveholding and non-slaveholding states would be admitted on a one-to-one basis. Southerners found their dominance in national politics gradually diminished with each passing decade. Northern states saw dramatic increases in population as European immigrants arrived in large numbers to take advantage of the growing number of factory jobs available and the vast areas of suitable farmland in the expanding western territories of the United States. With each decade, northern states increased their representation in the House of Representatives, and they used this increasing power base to launch new demands for protective tariffs and the abolition of slavery. Even the three-fifths status of slaves could not compensate for the growing disparity in populations.

The populations of southern states, with their commitment to a cotton economy cultivated on large plantations with slave labor, grew slowly. The absence of factories and the lack of available farmland held few attractions for new arrivals from Europe. Southern states were able to stymie many of the more extreme proposals of northern congressmen or to force such measures to be watered down through compromise. One final compromise between the agricultural South and the increasingly industrial North was reached when gold-rich California applied for admission as a state. Because of its location, California was bisected by the 36° 30′ line established by the Missouri Compromise, and a new compromise had to be reached. California would be admitted as a free state, but future states would be admitted only after a vote on the question by their residents. While this might upset the balance in the Senate, southern states were somewhat placated by the passage of the Fugitive Slave Act, which authorized slaveholders to recover their slaves who had escaped to the North, made northerners complicit in the act by requiring them to assist the slave hunters and imposed penalties on individuals who failed to comply. Suddenly, abolitionists were legally obligated to support the institution of slavery by this law, and runaways who were prominent in the antislavery movement became targets for slave hunters. Most northerners ignored the law or challenged it in court, but in 1857, the United States Supreme Court under Chief Justice Roger B. Taney, a southerner, ruled in the Dred Scott decision that slaves and former slaves were not and could not be citizens and therefore lacked standing in courts. The Compromise of 1850, the Fugitive Slave Law and the Dred Scott decision were the battle lines drawn, and leaders from both North and South let it be known that they had "gone this far, but we will go no further!"

The era of compromises had passed. What lay ahead for Americans was uncertain—either a peaceful dissolution of the Union would happen or a civil war would ensue. Assured of its dominance of the American economy through its production of cotton, the South was confident of success should secession from the Union lead to war. On the floor of the U.S. Senate, Senator James Henry Hammond of South Carolina declared in 1858, "You dare not make war upon cotton! No power on earth dares make war upon it. Cotton is king."

5

BLOCKADE RUNNERS, RIVER STEAMERS AND GUNBOATS

*A*lthough Senator James H. Hammond of South Carolina confidently predicted that the power of America's cotton exports was such that no one would dare to make war on it, his words rang hollow when on April 12, 1861, Confederate batteries opened fire on Union soldiers in Fort Sumter in Charleston Harbor when word was received that the Union forces would be reinforced by additional forces. To prevent that, Confederate general Pierre G.T. Beauregard ordered southern artillery batteries to reduce the fort and take possession of it. The American Civil War, the bloodiest war in the nation's history, had begun.

While the election of Abraham Lincoln, an antislavery Republican from Illinois, as president in 1860 was the immediate cause of the South's decision to secede, he was not a so-called Radical Republican intent on immediately ending the institution of slavery. Lincoln hoped that slavery would eventually die out as the nation moved more and more toward industrialization, although he deplored the dehumanization aspects of the institution. Despite his moderate stand on slavery, he was viewed as a Black Republican, and his election was considered the harbinger of a direct attack on the South, cotton and the institution of slavery.

Within weeks of the November 1860 election, southern states began organizing conventions to formalize secession. On February 8, 1861, delegates from seven southern states met in Montgomery, Alabama, and proclaimed the creation of the Confederate States of America.

Jefferson Davis of Mississippi was chosen as the provisional president of the new Confederate States of America. Davis had the difficult task of overseeing the formation of a new government and the establishment of an army and navy from scratch. *Courtesy of the Wynne Collection.*

These men immediately began writing a constitution and creating a new government. On February 18, Jefferson Davis of Mississippi was inaugurated as the provisional president of the breakaway republic. Following the outbreak of war, four additional southern states would join the Confederacy and the legislatures of two other slaveholding states passed resolutions declaring them to be members of the new nation. These two—Kentucky and Missouri—established new Confederate governments but were never fully controlled by southern forces. Although their claim to be part of the Confederacy was tenuous, they were allowed full representation in the Confederate Congress.

Several attempts at reaching a compromise were made in late 1860 and early 1861. The most famous of these was the proposed Crittenden Compromise, which would have created a constitutionally guaranteed permanent border between free states and slave states along the line of 36° 30′ and included six proposed constitutional amendments to assuage southern fears about the status of slavery in the future. The Crittenden Compromise failed in Congress. So, too, did other less public efforts to negotiate a workable compromise.

From the outset, both sides prepared for war. Federal arsenals were taken over by troops of the newly seceded states, and the arms they contained were distributed to state troops. State guards and militia groups began to coalesce around federal fortifications in the South, and those that were unmanned or lightly garrisoned were placed under state control. In Florida, Fort Clinch at Fernandina, Fort Marion at St. Augustine and the Chattahoochee Arsenal in the Panhandle fell to state troops without opposition. Key West and Fort Jefferson, far from the mainland, remained in federal hands. So, too, did Fort Pickens in Pensacola, although the Warrenton Naval Yard, Fort McRee and Fort Barrancas were captured without incident.

Along Florida's coasts, civilians took the lead in protecting the state from possible Union attacks and in aiding blockade runners by removing the lenses to the various lighthouses that guided ships at sea along the treacherous shoals and flats that surrounded the peninsula. From St. Augustine on the Atlantic to St. Marks on the Gulf, lighthouse after lighthouse went dark and their lenses either hidden away or transported to the mainland. The only lighthouses working by 1862 were the isolated lights on small tenders along the Keys from Miami to Fort Jefferson. Union secretary of the treasury Salmon P. Chase appealed to Gideon Welles, the secretary of the navy, for help in dealing with the crisis: "A band of lawless persons have recently attacked the light-house and destroyed or removed the expensive illuminating apparatus from the two important lights, Jupiter Inlet and Cape Florida, and the Department has been informed that the two important lights at Carysfort Reef and at Dry Bank, near Sombrero Key on the Florida Reefs, have been threatened." Chase's solution was simple: "Commander Pickering, lately the light-house inspector on that coast, is of the opinion (and in this opinion the Light-House Board fully concurs) that a small vessel properly armed, not drawing over 7 feet of water, could protect all the lights on the Florida Reefs and do other efficient service by cruising in the Hawk Channel between Cape Florida and Sombrero Key. There are, as will be seen by the Coast Survey charts, entrances through the reef from the Florida Reefs into Hawk Channel south of Cape Florida." Such a deployment would be appreciated, he argued, as he had "received numerous communications on this subject from merchants, presidents of insurance companies, and from other sources of the highest respectability."

Immediately after the Confederate assault on Fort Sumter, Lincoln issued a proclamation on April 15 calling for 75,000 men to serve three months to eliminate "combinations too powerful to be suppressed by the ordinary course of judicial proceedings, or by the powers vested in the marshals by law." The regular Union army, which had numbered about 16,000 men previously, would now number almost 100,000. On March 6, Lincoln's Confederate counterpart, Jefferson Davis, had issued a similar call for 100,000 volunteers to serve for a period of twelve months.

Following Virginia's secession, the Confederate capital moved from its provisional location in Montgomery to a permanent home in Richmond. The shift in the center of southern government also dictated a shift in overall strategy for the Confederate military. Departments were created to simplify the army's command structure and quickly identify the strengths of the individual armies of the Confederacy. In the first years of the war, the Confederacy fielded several armies with regional identifications—for

Lighthouses along the Florida Atlantic Coast suffered the loss of their lenses when pro-Confederate civilians took them and hid them until the war was over. *Courtesy of the Wynne Collection.*

example, the Army of Tennessee, the Army of Mississippi, the Army of Virginia—but the department to which Florida was assigned, the Department of Georgia, South Carolina and Florida, remained the same throughout the war. Within a department, a separate commander for each state was chosen.

The proximity of Richmond to Washington dictated Confederate strategy at first. To protect its new capital and to take advantage of existing roads and railroads as interior supply routes, the Army of Virginia quickly became the principal military force in the South. With only two exceptions when it invaded the North under Lee's leadership, the Army of Virginia operated within the boundaries of the state. It was the largest southern army and suffered the greatest number of casualties as the war progressed. Other southern armies also relied on interior lines of supply but operated in larger theaters of war. Facing a nation with greater resources and a larger population, Confederate leaders sought to maximize the effectiveness of their armies through a defensive-offensive strategy—that is, to rely on a strong defense and go on the offense only when the Union armies were weak or in retreat. When Confederate generals violated this principle, they invited disaster.

Following the bombardment of Fort Sumter on April 12, Abraham Lincoln imposed a blockade of southern ports on April 19, 1861. Though initially limited in its scope, by July the blockade extended along the entire coastlines of the Confederacy. The overall Union strategy was summed up by Winfield Scott, the general-in-chief of the federal army, on May 3, 1861, when he stated,

> *We rely greatly on the sure operation of a complete blockade of the Atlantic and Gulf ports soon to commence. In connection with such blockade we propose a powerful movement down the Mississippi to the ocean, with a cordon of posts at proper points, and the capture of Forts Jackson and Saint Philip; the object being to clear out and keep open this great line of communication in connection with the strict blockade of the seaboard, so as to envelop the insurgent States and bring them to terms with less bloodshed than by any other plan.*

This so-called Anaconda Plan was fraught with peril for the United States. First, the concept of imposing a total blockade violated recognized international law, particularly regarding the rights of neutral nations. Second, blockades were usually imposed only during declared wars, and the Union had clearly designated its fight with the Confederacy as an insurrection. Third, the effect of a total blockade would dramatically and negatively affect the economies of neutral nations. Last, the proclamation of a blockade in 1861 was judged by such nations as illegal because when it was first declared, the Union lacked the ships necessary

Right: General Winfield Scott, the aging general-in-chief of the U.S. army, decided the demands of fighting a new war were too much for him, so he resigned his position. Before he left, however, he formulated a successful strategy for fighting the war. His Anaconda Plan became the basis of Union campaigns. *Courtesy of the Wynne Collection.*

Below: The Anaconda Plan called for the Union to establish an effective blockade of Confederate coasts and split the Confederacy along its major water routes. *Courtesy of the Wynne Collection.*

to enforce it. For Europeans, the Union blockade was simply a paper blockade that they were expected to enforce voluntarily on themselves. According to the Declaration of Paris, an 1856 treaty that defined the rights of neutrals and the requirements for a blockade, any recognized blockade had to be effective to be legal, and such was not the case for the United States.

By July 1861, Union engineers and naval planners had produced an extensive report on when, where and how the blockade could be enforced. Maps, navigation aids, warehouse facilities, weather predictions and manpower needs for occupying ports or patrolling coastlines and rivers were clearly spelled out. Fortifications and possible Confederate artillery batteries were marked, and potential resistance by locals was also noted. A plan for imposing a blockade was created but lacked one crucial element to be effective.

In 1861, the U.S. Navy could claim only seventy-six vessels of all types, which was scarcely enough to patrol the roughly two thousand miles of Confederate coastline and still aid Union armies operating along navigable rivers. According to Nick Wynne and Joe Crankshaw in *Florida Civil War Blockades*, "Of these ships, only forty-two were in adequate repair to be used. Of the forty-two, thirty Federal ships were on station in foreign waters, which left twelve for use as blockaders. Of these twelve, only four ships, which carried a complement of 280 men and twenty-five guns, were pressed into immediate service." They continued,

Twenty-four of these were steam powered. By the end of that year, an additional seventy-nine steamers and fifty-eight sailing vessels had been purchased. The number of sailors had been increased from 7,900 in January 1861 to more than 24,000 in December 1861. By the end of the war in 1865, the Union navy had expanded to some seven hundred ships and an additional sixty ironclad coastal monitors. Of these ships, about six hundred were assigned to blockade duty along the Confederate coasts, with about four hundred on duty at any one time. The remaining ships were assigned to various overseas stations tracking and attacking Confederate commerce raiders. At any one time, approximately 86 percent of the total Union naval strength was devoted to enforcing the blockade. When the war ended in 1865, the Union navy reported some 51,000 sailors and officers on duty and a total of more than 132,000 men having served for some period of the war.

Stephen Russell Mallory, a former U.S. senator and a resident of Key West, was appointed as the Confederate secretary of the navy. He was charged with building a fleet of oceanic and riverine warships. *Drawing by Jeanette Boughner in the Lewis N. Wynne Collection.*

If additional ships were required to support armies operating along the Mississippi River, it would take time to purchase newer ships from civilian sources or build them in naval shipyards. Thus, for a full year the scarcity of available Union naval vessels amounted to the paper blockade other nations claimed it was. Instead of Union ships effectively blockading the southern coasts, the North found that the South was responsible for its strongest enforcement.

In response to the blockade, Confederate leaders chose to rely on the power of King Cotton to bring international recognition as a viable and separate nation from European powers like France and Great Britain, along with the German states and Russia. Because these countries were the major consumers of southern cotton, Confederate leaders sought to coerce them into supporting their new government as a belligerent nation by withholding cotton and idling the textile plants in those nations. On the surface, such a strategy seemed viable. By the late 1850s, southern cotton accounted for 77 percent of the cotton consumed in Britain, 90 percent of that used in French factories, 60 percent of the cotton spun in German factories and 92 percent of that used in Russian factories.

Florida governor John Milton prohibited the export of cotton in 1861, a decision that was quickly adopted by the central Confederate government. Milton issued orders to Colonel R.F. Floyd on November 25, 1861, to prevent blockade runners from leaving Apalachicola with cargoes of cotton. Milton's instructions were specific: "Permit no vessel with cotton, to leave Apalachicola; issue an order prohibiting it; if attempted, sink the vessel. Arrest and place in close confinement any and every individual who shall attempt to ship cotton from Apalachicola. With regard to other descriptions of cargo, exercise a sound discretion." Floyd put Milton's prohibition into effect immediately and, on November 27, reported, "Your orders respecting cotton shall be strictly observed. Turpentine is also forbidden to be sent abroad. I learned that 300 bales of cotton had lately arrived here for shipment. I will order it back to the

John Milton, an ardent secessionist, served as Florida's wartime governor. Among his first actions as governor was to impose an embargo on cotton and naval stores normally shipped from Florida ports. *Courtesy of Florida Memory.*

river at once." Within a few months, it was thought, the shortage of southern cotton would idle European textile factories, and the thousands of unemployed workers would pressure the governments of these nations to break the blockade through force and lend military assistance to the Confederacy to protect their source of cotton.

From the beginning, the reliance on cotton diplomacy was a failure. In 1861, European cotton warehouses were overflowing with southern cotton and mills continued to operate. By late 1862, these supplies were greatly diminished and many mills closed. Workers demanded that governments find solutions to the crisis, but the solutions they found were not the ones anticipated by the Confederacy. Instead of risking a war with the United States, Europeans relied on new sources—Brazil, India and Egypt—of cotton. Although the quality of Indian and Egyptian cotton did not match the excellence of southern cotton, it could be used.

By the middle of 1862, the South had abandoned King Cotton diplomacy as ineffective and promoted the use of blockade runners to ferry cotton to Europe in exchange for critically needed supplies of arms and ammunition. The limited supplies seized from federal arsenals in early 1861 did not approach the requirements an army of thousands of soldiers needed. The war quickly became a longer and larger conflict than had been predicted by both sides, and the Confederacy's need for arms, ammunition and other critical military supplies continually increased. Although factories were started that could meet some of this need, the lack of raw materials and manpower did not provide enough of an industrial base to meet the demand. The institution of slavery was not structured to make a quick conversion from an agricultural economy to a factory system.

What of Florida? Despite the seizures of Fort Clinch and Fort Marion and the occupation of Pensacola, little attention had been paid to the state by the Confederate government. The bulk of Confederate troops in the state were state troops, commanded and supplied by Florida. The peninsula was divided into the districts of Middle and Eastern Florida,

Robert E. Lee made the decision to abandon the coastal fortifications of Florida and protect the interior with small mobile forces. *Courtesy of the Wynne Collection.*

with a centralized headquarters at Live Oak, and the Panhandle remained under the command of the Confederate army occupying Pensacola until they evacuated that city in May 1862. When Robert E. Lee was appointed commander of the Department of Georgia, South Carolina and East Florida on November 8, 1861, he quickly established what was to be the Confederate strategy for the state—the ports, with the single exception of Apalachicola, were too poorly defended to resist opposing Union attacks and should be abandoned. Union movements in the west along the Mississippi had placed severe strains on available Confederate manpower, he wrote to General J.H. Trapier, who commanded Confederate forces in Florida on March 13, 1862, saying,

> *The Secretary* [of War has]…*directed that the only troops to be retained in Florida were those employed in the defense of the Apalachicola, and I wished you to understand that our necessities might limit us to the defense*

of that avenue through Florida into Georgia. My own opinion and desire is to hold the interior of the State, if your force will be adequate, the Saint John's River, as well as the Apalachicola. I do not think you will be able to hold Tampa Bay, and the small force posted at Saint Augustine serves only as an invitation to attack.

Federal forces fighting along the Tennessee River were poised to move along the Mississippi River and split the Confederacy. Such a catastrophic event had to be stopped, wrote Judah P. Benjamin, the Confederate secretary of war, but "we can only do this by withdrawing troops from the seaboard. You are therefore requested to withdraw all such forces as are now employed in the defense of the seaboard of Florida, taking proper steps to secure the guns and munitions of war, and to send forward the troops to Tennessee." On January 31, 1862, General J.H. Trapier, the commander of the Districts of Middle and Eastern Florida, reported that he had a total of 3,348 men in his command, including officers. A year later, that number had dwindled to only 1,561 men and officers. Despite their small numbers, the Confederates managed to keep the much larger Union army and navy at bay and prevented the conquest of Florida.

Once the Union navy began implementing the Anaconda Plan, coastal towns in Florida fell rapidly. In March 1862, a Union fleet commanded by flag officer Samuel F. DuPont quickly took control of Fernandina, which had largely been abandoned by its populace, and Jacksonville, which offered no opposition. St. Augustine, which also offered no opposition and whose population was welcoming though divided over its support of the Union and the Confederacy, was occupied. Union officers were amazed that Fernandina and Fort Clinch were taken with no opposition. In their opinion, Fort Clinch and its defenses were well constructed and could have resisted effectively. DuPont reported the ease with which the city fell:

A few scattered musket shots were fired from the town by the flying enemy, when it was discovered that a railroad train was about to start. Commander Drayton, on board the Ottawa…*chased this train for 2 miles and fired several shells at it, aiming at the locomotive, some of which took effect. It is reported that the Hon. David Yulee, late a Senator of the United States from the State of Florida, escaped from this train and took to the bush.*

The 1,500 Confederate soldiers stationed at Fort Clinch retreated into the countryside.

Samuel F. DuPont chaired an 1861 Union naval committee to assess Confederate ports in Florida and determine those that should be captured and those that could be ignored. *Courtesy of the Library of Congress.*

St. Augustine, protected by Fort Marion, was also taken without a fight. Confederate troops stationed there evacuated the city and made their way by boat to New Smyrna, which remained a major entry port for blockade runners throughout the war. Union authorities in St. Augustine had to contend with strong pro-Confederate sympathies from some citizens, and although residents adjusted to living with federal troops over time, some Augustinians remained loyal to the Confederacy and supplied information to southern forces operating along the St. Johns.

Jacksonville, a small village on the banks of the St. Johns, quickly fell to Union gunboats when Confederate forces retreated. Over the course of the next three years, the city would be occupied four times by Union forces. Control of Jacksonville was important for several reasons. First, its location dominated the St. Johns near the mouth of the river; second, Jacksonville became the center of pro-Union sympathizers in northeast Florida; and third, the city also became a major destination for hundreds of escaped slaves seeking the protection of Union forces. Because of its strategic location, Jacksonville and nearby Mayport became centers for federal riverine operations along the St. Johns and its tributaries. The city provided a safe location for gunboats to refuel and resupply. To counter this Union advantage, Confederate engineers sowed torpedoes and mines in the river channels. While such devices were seldom exploded by federal ships, their presence and the fear factor they produced had a demoralizing effect on Union sailors. Fears took on a reality when the troop carrier and supply ship *Maple Leaf* hit a torpedo on April 1, 1864, and sank.

Although the Union forces took control of Jacksonville four times, Unionists, who had welcomed the federal forces and convened a conference to pass resolutions stating their loyalty to the United States, found it necessary to evacuate Jacksonville when it was abandoned by them. Confederate forces were never strong enough to take the city and hold it. When General Pierre G.T. Beauregard arrived in the state after the major Union defeat at Olustee in February 1864 with the stated goal of taking and holding Jacksonville, he soon realized that Confederate resources were simply too little to do so. Although unable to wrest Jacksonville from the Union permanently, Confederate forces mounted a continuous campaign of guerrilla warfare against Union troops. Small groups of federal troops that ventured out from the city were subject to capture or death by southern units. Captain J.J. Dickison, known as Florida's Swamp Fox, gained legendary status for his exploits in defeating the groups of Union troops who left the safe confines of Jacksonville, St. Augustine or Palatka.

The presence of Union forces in Jacksonville proved to be a magnet for escaping slaves from northeastern Florida plantations and towns. When the federal government decided to create the United States Colored Troops, the contrabands in the city provided many recruits. The Union navy also recruited sailors from the contraband population. Although African Americans had served in the Union army from the start of the war, a formal order creating the USCT was issued on May 22, 1863, and active recruitment began. By July 1863, enough African American soldiers had been recruited in Florida to form the Fourth USCT Regiment at Fernandina. From February until March 1864, the city was occupied by African American soldiers.

The Confederate decision to abandon the major ports on the coasts was the correct move because the small number of state troops could concentrate their efforts at controlling the rivers that led to the interior of the peninsula. Lee and Benjamin's fear that the Apalachicola River "by which the enemy's gunboats

Confederate captain J.J. Dickison terrorized Union troops along the St. Johns with a small group of cavalry. His constant raids and daring escapades earned him the sobriquet "Florida's Swamp Fox." *Courtesy of the Wynne Collection.*

may penetrate far into the State of Georgia" proved unfounded. While it was true that the Apalachicola River, which connected with the Flint and Chattahoochee Rivers, went to the heart of Georgia and northern Alabama, it never became a focus of any major Union attack simply because it was too narrow and had too many bends and curves, all of which offered numerous opportunities for hidden Confederate artillery batteries. When the Union navy made an appearance at Apalachicola in March 1862, the sailors found that all the Confederate soldiers and most of the town's population had fled before the arrival of the ship. Governor John Milton had ordered the evacuation of the town and transferred the 650 soldiers to Fernandina in anticipation of an attack there. Only a dozen or so white families remained, along with a few Spanish fishermen and a small number of slaves, and of these, reported Captain H.S. Stellwagen of the USS *Mercedita*, "many…are inclined for the Union, but are not at liberty to speak. Threats have often been made to hang or to starve them as damn Yankees, traitors to the South. In this category stand also many of the fishermen who have not enlisted in their army. Threats are also made to burn the whole town if they hold intercourse with us."

Apalachicola would be taken and abandoned several times over the course of the war by Union and Confederate troops. To prevent Union attacks upriver, fortifications were erected at Ricco's Bluff and obstructions placed in the river.

The Union's control of Apalachee Bay did not go unchallenged by the Confederacy. In May 1864, the CSS *Chattahoochee*, a state-of-the-art steam-powered gunboat built in the Confederate Naval Yard in Saffold, Georgia, began making its way down the Apalachicola River with the intent of sweeping the bay clean of Union blockaders. Unfortunately, while waiting for the river to rise while at the dock at Chattahoochee, Florida, the ship's boiler exploded, killing or injuring a number of crewmen. Although the *Chattahoochee* was raised and towed back to the naval yard for repairs, it never participated in any further expeditions and was destroyed before it could be captured by Union forces in 1865.

What was true for the Apalachicola River could be said of most of the small rivers in Florida. Only the broad St. Johns offered Union gunboats the space needed to maneuver and avoid deadly shore batteries. The best example of how the narrow, twisting rivers of Florida allowed much smaller Confederate forces to prevent a Union conquest of the state can be found in the case of the *Columbine*, a small rivercraft used to transport troops and supplies. On May 23, 1864, a small Confederate force led by Captain J.J. Dickison caught the *Columbine* in a narrow tributary of the St. Johns River at Horse Landing. Employing cannon and small arms fire, he disabled the boat and forced its surrender. Dickison's small force of some thirty or so men engaged in a forty-five-minute battle that resulted in tremendous losses for the Union boat. "We captured in this engagement," he reported, "7 commissioned officers and 1 claiming to be a noncombatant, 9 seamen, and 47 enlisted [N]egroes. Number killed and drowned, about 25. Of the [N]egro troops, Captain Daniels and 5 [N]egroes were wounded, 3 of which are mortal. Among the killed was a lieutenant of the naval service. After the surrender several of the men jumped overboard and swam for the opposite shore, but most of them were drowned."

The narrow, twisting nature of Florida's rivers provided excellent opportunities for Confederate troops to harass Union gunboats and supply vessels with guerrilla tactics or by the use of torpedoes and mines. *Courtesy of the* Florida Times Union.

The Confederates' decision to deliberately curtail the flow of cotton from southern ports for almost a year gave the federal government time to purchase or build needed ships, train new recruits and organize the ships into effective squadrons to patrol specific areas of the coasts. Although the self-imposed cotton embargo reduced the numbers of ships exiting southern ports, it did not prevent governments from purchasing or hiring ships or encouraging individuals to become blockade runners to bring in needed arms, medicines and ammunition. On November 29, 1861, Governor Milton asked Stephen R. Mallory, the Confederate secretary of the navy and a Florida native, about how inclusive the embargo was on exports. "Shall vessels be permitted to go from Apalachicola," Milton inquired, "risking the blockade, with turpentine, to procure acids for telegraphic operations, coffee, etc., from Havana? Vessels ready and stopped by my order. Answer immediately." There was no reason, Mallory replied, why ships loaded with such cargoes should not be allowed to exit the port.

Blockade runners were the answer to the Confederacy's problem of finding quantities of arms necessary to fighting a war. From 1861 to 1865, some 600,000 stands of arms were imported, together with 3 million pounds

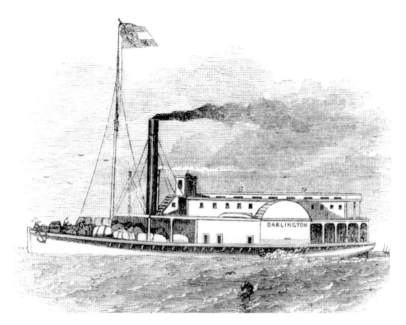

The *Darlington*, an early blockade runner carrying cotton to Europe, was captured by Union ships and eventually placed in the service of the Federal navy. As blockade running became more profitable and steam technology improved, sidewheelers gave way to screw-driven and faster ships. *Courtesy of the Wynne Collection.*

The blockade runner *Robert E. Lee* was built specifically for penetrating the Union blockade with valuable cargo, and the ship incorporated the latest in naval design. Captured by Federal ships, it was pressed into Union service and renamed the USS *Fort Donelson*. *Courtesy of the U.S. Naval Historical Center.*

of lead, large numbers of field artillery, vast amounts of cloth and leather for uniforms and 2.5 million pounds of saltpeter—a critical ingredient in the manufacture of gunpowder—all of which arrived via blockade runners. Fully 60 percent of the arms and ammunition expended by Confederate forces during the war came from European manufacturers, without which the South would have not been able to sustain any kind of large-scale or extended campaign against the Union.

From the beginning, the Union blockade was porous, and enterprising individuals loaded cargoes of cotton and attempted to pass through the ever-tightening Union cordon. The prospect of making a great deal of money fast was a lure that drew risk-takers aplenty. From small barges that hugged the coastline and carried only two or three bales of cotton to larger ports to fully rigged schooners capable of carrying one to two hundred bales, the enormous profits to be made provided the motivation for many people to make the attempt. Return voyages with cargoes of critically needed military equipment and luxury items brought even greater profits and proved irresistible.

In his 1994 article "The Hapless Anaconda: Union Blockade 1861–1865" in the *Concord Review*, attorney Jochem H. Tans, using statistical data assembled by earlier historians Frank L. Owsley and Marcus Price, argued that the blockade was a practical failure but a superb psychological success. According to Tans, 85.3 percent of the 6,316 attempts to run the blockade were successful. For fast steam-powered ships, the success rate was even higher—2,526 out of 2,743 attempts—92.1 percent. For slower sailing vessels, 4 out of every 5 attempts—80.2 percent—were successful.

In Great Britain, companies dedicated to running the blockade were formed by investors looking for easy profits. Operating like normal shipping companies, the newly formed operations agreed to carry whatever cargo that was assigned, bought maritime insurance for their loads, invested huge sums in acquiring the fastest and newest ships and hired professional crews. Author Philip Van Doren Stern reported that such companies often paid 500 to 1,000 percent dividends to investors in this "golden bonanza." Although about 1,500 blockade runners were captured, the loss of a ship and its cargo had little effect on profits because most operators were willing to pay high premiums for insurance against losses. Insurance costs usually ran about 45 to 50 percent of the value of the ship and its cargo. Stern demonstrated the enormous profits that could be made by a single successful run to and from a southern port:

PROFITS AND COSTS
SUCCESSFUL BLOCKADE RUN ROUNDTRIP

	Costs
Wages (officers and crew)	$18,840
Food (passengers and crew)	5,700
Coal, oil	5,800
Insurance, pilot fees, miscellaneous	12,625
Risk Insurance	37,500
Total Expense	**$80,465**
Earnings	
800 bales of government cotton	$40,000
800 bales of privately owned cotton	40,000
Return freight for owners	40,000
Return freight for government	40,000
Passenger fares	12,000
Total Earnings	**$172,000**
Profit	**$91,535**

A letter from Alfred Judah to his father in 1863 requesting permission to invest £100 in the trade was intercepted by Union authorities and demonstrated the appeal blockade running held for would-be entrepreneurs. "There are men here who are making immense fortunes by shipping goods to Dixie, and on an average four out of every six vessels that start to run the blockade succeed, and goods of all kinds are worth ridiculous prices there," he wrote. The likelihood was that most blockade runners would get through the Union net if they took precautions:

> Six steamers left this port last week to run the blockade, and we have heard of the safe arrival in Dixie of five of them.... The way in which it is managed is this: They carry no lights on board, the ships are painted lead color and are hardly visible at 100 yards off, and they only go when there is no moon and the nights are very dark. Sailing vessels are more frequently caught and the goods confiscated, for they cannot choose their time as a steamer can.

What kind of goods was Judah seeking to invest in? "Salt, for example, is one of the most paying things to send in," he wrote. "Here in Nassau it is only worth 60 cents a bushel, but in Charleston brings at auction from $80 to $100 in Confederate money, but as Confederate money is no good out of the Confederacy they send back cotton or turpentine, which, if it reaches here, is worth proportionally as much here as the salt is there." The returns were worth the risk, he promised: "I see nothing to prevent my making something handsome." After all, "There is one man here who commenced in this line of business as soon as the war broke out and he has made over $2,000,000."

Not all southerners were enthusiastic about blockade running. E.S. Dargan, a citizen of Mobile, wrote to Confederate secretary of war James A. Seddon in June 1863 expressing his feelings that blockade runners should be restrained because "I see that the running the blockade unless restrained will ruin us forever." The money received, he continued, "most of it is laid out in brandies, wines, and flimsy gewgaws that bring exorbitant prices, but little in articles that produce substantial good. But besides this it is corrupting our people; it is turning all their hearts and souls to speculating."

Because of the long stretch of coasts that needed to be patrolled, the Union divided its blockading fleet into three squadrons assigned to specific areas. The North Atlantic Blockading Squadron, based in Port Royal, South Carolina, assumed responsibility from Cumberland Island north, while the South Atlantic Blockading Squadron and the East Gulf Blockading Squadron enforced the blockade along Florida's Atlantic and Gulf of Mexico coasts. To motivate Union sailors to greater efforts in stopping runners, the Union pursued a policy of awarding shares of the value of a capture to the officers and crew of the successful ship. Captured ships, along with their cargoes, were taken to Key West to be sold at public auction, which meant that sailors and officers of Union ships often received considerable amounts of money for their efforts. If several ships were involved in a single capture, the prize money would be shared accordingly.

Captured ships were either purchased by the Union navy for use as blockading ships or sold to private investors as prizes of war, which meant that many of the captured vessels were returned to blockade running by their new owners. Union secretary of the navy Gideon Welles noted this unfortunate fact in a letter to Rear Admiral Theodorus Bailey in June 1863. "It is quite likely," he wrote, "that most of the steamers condemned and sold

The lack of enough ships to enforce the blockade during 1861 and 1862 forced the Union navy to purchase existing ships or build more, which allowed the Union to construct or buy a new fleet of modern steam-powered, screw-driven and iron-hulled vessels, such as the USS *Memphis. Courtesy of the U.S. Naval Historical Center.*

at Key West will go into the hands of the rebels or the blockade runners unless purchased by the Government." Certainly, blockade runners had their agents attend the public auctions and purchase cargoes and ships that had been captured.

Key West, the site of the admiralty court where captures from the south Atlantic and Gulf of Mexico were taken, was, despite its continuous occupation by the Union army and navy, a hotbed of Confederate sympathizers. During the lead-up to the war, most of the prominent citizens of the city had expressed pro-secession feelings, and local newspapers were unabashed in their support of establishing a southern confederacy. The city produced several leading figures in the South's military, including Stephen R. Mallory, the Confederate secretary of the navy. Very early, the Union had reinforced its garrisons at Fort Taylor and Fort Jefferson against the possibility of an attempt by the Confederate army to seize the city and harbor. So pervasive was the pro-South sentiment in Key West and so apprehensive were Union fears about an attack, on September 6, 1861, Major William H. French, who commanded Fort Taylor, issued an order that citizens who failed to swear allegiance to the United States and their relatives were to be removed from the island. The order continued, "This will also apply to their families and the families of those who have left the island to join the Confederate States."

In addition to a possible Confederate attack, the Union naval commanders at Key West were quickly introduced to another possible cause to abandon that strategic harbor—yellow fever. The cause of this tropical disease was unknown to medical practitioners at the time, but it was recognized as a killer. Key West was subject to periodic outbreaks—1823, 1854, 1856, 1860, 1861, 1862 and 1864—and despite efforts by military authorities to control the disease by enforcing cleanups of the city, it persisted. Union ships at sea also experienced severe outbreaks of yellow fever because their patrols along the coasts took them into swampy areas where the anopheles mosquitoes lived and bred unchecked. So bad was the outbreak in 1864, the headquarters of the Union blockading squadrons was moved from Key West to Tampa.

The experience of the crew of the USS *James S. Chambers* was typical of what happened when fever struck a ship at sea. In August 1864, the *Chambers* was patrolling the barrier islands along the Indian River Lagoon when the fever first struck the crew. Within days, the ship's commander, Luther Nickerson, wrote in the ship's log,

> *To-day we have a sick and binnacle list of 38, over two-thirds of our number. Three of my officers were taken last night and are very sick. I have lost four men to death since the 5th Instance, burying one this morning (First Class Boy William Wilkinson). There are a number of others I have but little hopes of. The few remaining who are not sick are worn down by nursing the sick. I can barely raise enough men to man a boat. I do not think it is yellow fever, but never saw persons suffer so much and become so reduced in such short time. The symptoms are much the same as that disease.*

Florida waters were dangerous in and of themselves.

Sailors in the blockading squadrons endured long weeks of tedium at sea between encounters with blockade runners, and as a result, they turned their attention to destroying the numerous saltworks along the coasts. Salt was used in food preservation, gunpowder manufacture, seasoning and for a myriad of other purposes. It was so scarce in southern states that it became the single most valuable cargo, other than arms and ammunition, for blockade runners to bring into the South. In 1862, salt sold for ten dollars a bushel or twenty cents a pound; in 1864, the market price had doubled, but salt was hard to find; and by 1865, the soil beneath smokehouses in the South had been excavated in searches for residual salt.

The coasts of Florida proved a cheap and reliable source of salt, easily recovered through natural evaporation or by boiling seawater in huge iron

Saltworks were essential for the Confederacy. Located on coastal areas, they provided salt for food preservation and other critical necessities. Federal blockaders destroyed them where they found them, but the simple works, consisting of boilers fueled by wood fires, were quickly rebuilt. *Courtesy of Florida Memory.*

pans. Some states without ready access to the sea hired men to go to the Florida coasts and start operations to produce salt. The need for salt was so great, men employed in salt production were exempted from conscription in the Confederate army. Florida governor John Milton wrote to Florida members of the Confederate Congress expressing his concerns about allowing such exemptions:

> *Since the enactment of the conscript act many able-bodied men from adjacent States and this State have repaired to the coast of Florida, under the pretense of making salt, and to be secure in their labor some have been treacherous enough to hold intercourse with the enemy; others have been lazy loungers, more anxious to avoid military service than to make salt.*

Despite Milton's concerns about draft dodgers, the practice continued, and hundreds of small saltworks could be found on the Atlantic and Gulf Coasts.

The Civil War in Florida was a naval war. Union forces, though much larger than their Confederate opponents, mostly confined their efforts to areas of the coasts or major rivers. The vast expanses of open land and an openly hostile civilian population presented too much of a challenge to occupy. When the Union army undertook land operations outside the protection of naval gunships—the Battles of Olustee and Natural Bridge—they proved disastrous. Confederate troops, though few, were able to move freely in the countryside among a friendly population, quickly abandon fixed fortifications in the face of enemy assaults and not hampered by long supply lines or heavy equipment. Utilizing guerrilla tactics, they successfully prevented Union forces from penetrating the heartland of Florida.

Because of the limited nature of the conflict in Florida, the state suffered little overall destruction. Indeed, most Florida ports, left uncontested, were in much better condition when the war ended than they had been in 1860. To accommodate the large number of Union ships and army units, major ports had been expanded and improved by Union engineers. In addition, the use of steam-powered boats on the St. Johns River and other rivers demonstrated the viability of riverine transport for peaceful purposes. Overall, the Civil War, like other American wars, proved beneficial to Florida in the long run.

6

RAILROADS, TOURISTS
AND NEW HARBORS

1865–1900

*W*ith the collapse of the Confederate States in April 1865, the old regime of large cotton plantations and a cash crop economy was gone. Floridians, many destitute because all Confederate currency and bonds were worthless, desperately sought new ways to earn their living. Industries such as fishing and citrus cultivation, which had received only passing attention during the antebellum period, suddenly took on a new importance. So, too, did cattle ranching, lumbering and naval stores operations. Although new railroad construction on the peninsula promised easier routes of transportation in the future, Florida's harbors, saved from destruction by the Confederate decision not to contest them in the war, provided the most expeditious means of getting products to market. Old harbors, like Fernandina, St. Augustine and Mayport, were consigned to secondary roles, while new harbors, like Cedar Key, Jacksonville, Bagdad and Punta Rassa, took on a new importance. The ports of Pensacola and Key West experienced an increase in the tonnage of cargoes and ships that used them, and the improvements made to accommodate Union warships proved equally of value for commercial ships.

Tourism also emerged as a mainstay of the state's economy. Although Florida had seen some seasonal visitors at places like White Springs, Fernandina and St. Augustine before the war, the rise of a new class of ultrawealthy robber barons and a well-to-do middle class greatly expanded the numbers of people who had money and were willing to spend it on leisure activities. The prewar wealthy classes had focused on the grand tour of European countries, but the rapid expansion of the United States westward brought attention to the abundance of unique flora and fauna, historical sites and other attractions to be seen and experienced at home. The American West, however, was still a dangerous place to visit in the years immediately after the end of the war. But Florida was safe!

Tourists were not the only newcomers to Florida. The three wars between the United States and the Seminole Nation ended in 1857, and settlers from southern and northern states, taking advantage of the liberal terms of the several Homestead Acts, claimed their stakes in the open territory of central and southern Florida. A byproduct of the Seminole Wars had been the exploration and surveying of most of the previously unsettled portions of the state to the south of present-day Orlando and Tampa, and the string of forts erected at critical points demonstrated that such lands could be brought under control and made productive.

White southerners, many seeking to escape the devastation of the war in older areas, saw Florida as a land of fresh opportunities and as a place to escape the restrictions of Reconstruction imposed by Union occupation. Some sought lands in the state to escape the results of emancipation. Selling what they had left of their prewar properties, they moved to Florida to begin again.

Former slaves were also attracted to Florida's open public land that had been set aside for settlement for freedmen and Unionists under the terms of the Southern Homestead Act of 1866. This law, which required Congress to override two vetoes by President Andrew Johnson, was aimed at providing land for Black people, who had emerged from slavery with little more than the clothes on their backs. Although the special exemptions were only in place for a year, or until January 1, 1867, opposition by state and local officials who refused to enforce the law, coupled with violence by local whites and a lack of cash, prevented large numbers of freedmen from taking advantage of the law. Of the more than forty-six million acres of land available in Florida, Alabama, Arkansas, Louisiana and Mississippi, only around 6,500 claims to the available 160-acre plots were filed in the five states, and of these few, only about 1,000 deeds were eventually recorded.

The 1870 Census showed that Florida's African American population increased an astounding 46.29 percent. The census also revealed that many Black people left the rural areas of the state and migrated to the cities, where they found employment in a variety of jobs that had previously been closed to them. Unfortunately, the lack of cash resources forced thousands of the formerly enslaved back into the agricultural economy of Florida under the

Following the end of the Civil War, African Americans in Florida were forced to labor as tenant farmers, sharecroppers and involuntarily as leased workers through the convict lease system. Private contractors often used this form of forced labor to construct new roads throughout the state. *Courtesy of the Wynne Collection.*

exploitative systems of sharecropping and tenant farming, while thousands more entered the naval stores industries. For Florida counties with large African American populations, little change came about after emancipation because what emerged to take the place of chattel slavery was just another form of enslavement, one that used debt as its binder, with an equally odious name, *peonage*. Still other African Americans were returned to a system of slavery through the convict lease system.

FLORIDA POPULATION GROWTH, 1870–1900

YEAR	POPULATION	% OF GROWTH
1870	187,748	33.7
1880	269,493	43.5
1890	391,422	45.2
1900	528,542	35.0

United States Census Schedules, 1870–1900

With little physical damage from the Civil War, Florida was primed for a rapid expansion of population and industry in the postwar period. First, the availability of land, coupled with a semitropical climate, encouraged the development of citrus production, truck farming and cattle ranching. Although individuals in the counties in the northern part of the state, closely tied to the economies of Georgia, Alabama and Mississippi, continued to cling to the production of cotton and tobacco, newly settled areas saw much more diverse economies emerge.

Second, the rapid postwar construction of roads, new harbors and railroads provided safe and reliable means to service out-of-state markets economically. In 1860, Florida had only one railroad that crossed the peninsula. Although the railway was of little value during the war because Union forces occupied both terminals of the line, its builder, David Levy Yulee, rebuilt the railroad after the war and quickly resumed operations. Over the next two decades, Yulee was joined by other railroad barons like Henry Flagler, Peter Demens, Henry Plant and William Dudley Chipley in creating rail networks that crisscrossed the state. As the railroads extended their lines in all directions, new towns and harbors were created. While the tourist hotels built by these men and their companies received the most publicity, the connections they provided from the interior of Florida to ports on the Atlantic Ocean and Gulf of Mexico would be of the most value. New industries, particularly phosphate mining, took advantage of the railroads to transport huge quantities of this natural fertilizer to Florida harbors and from there to markets around the world. From a paltry 500 miles of tracks in 1880, Florida could boast of an astounding 2,489 miles by the end of the decade, an increase of 480 percent. Railroad companies became some of the largest landholders in Florida because of the state and federal policies of granting alternating sections of land to them as a means of encouraging more construction and of subsidizing the costs involved. Once they had acquired the land, railroads faced the problem of selling their holdings to convert land into profits.

Railroads, however, were not in the forefront of the postwar settlement of Florida. Instead, boats in assorted sizes and shapes were used to bring settlers and goods to the lower half of Florida and to the interior of the state. Along the East Coast, settlement proved to be much easier than on the Gulf Coast. The stretches of open water and the numerous small bays and harbors that had once provided blockade runners safe havens proved useful for unloading passengers and freight. The system of roads along the coast amounted to little more than trails originally used by Native Americans, and virtually no

Henry Flagler (*pictured*) and Henry Plant were the most notable railroad entrepreneurs in post–Civil War Florida. Flagler's Florida East Coast Railway extended the length of the state's Atlantic Coast, while Plant's roads crossed the state and extended down the Gulf Coast. *Courtesy of Florida Memory.*

developed system of infrastructure existed. The East Coast, however, was fortunate to have the St. Johns River, which stretched for 310 miles south from Jacksonville, paralleled the coast and had many tributaries to provide entrée to Central Florida. The St. Johns, the Ocklawaha, the Wekiva and the Econlockhatchee Rivers became the superhighways of the day as large and small steamboats hauled freight and passengers to the interior of the peninsula. So complete was this transportation network that by the mid-1880s, it was possible to board a steamboat in Enterprise, the former seat of Volusia County and the major southern terminal of the St. Johns, and make a continuous journey by boat to New York City.

Closer to the Atlantic Coast, the Tomoka and Halifax Rivers provided easy access to Ormond, Daytona and New Smyrna. From New Smyrna, the protected waters of the Mosquito Inlet allowed an easy journey to the Indian River Lagoon, a 156-mile-long, placid, non-tidal, although shallow, water highway from Volusia County to present-day Jupiter. In 1870, the U.S. Census Bureau listed only 260 hardy souls occupying the coast between Titusville and modern Miami. Some were adventurers, some were individuals with tainted pasts and some were hopefuls who saw opportunities to create a better life for their families. Most settlers subsisted off the plentiful fish and animals that were native to the region, supplemented by small gardens carved out of the wilderness. Small groups of Native Americans roamed the area, stopping occasionally at isolated homesteads to trade furs and meats for simple staples.

By the end of the decade, great changes had come to the Indian River Lagoon, and greater changes would occur in the 1880s. Seeking to recapture the excitement of combat, veterans of the Union and Confederate armies sought new thrills from the dangers of the Florida wild. Some hardy individuals and small groups of tourists, fueled by tales of daring explorers in Africa and Asia, eagerly embraced the opportunities to confront the unknown in the primeval jungles of Florida. No theme parks, no artificial zoos and no frills. Tourists came to see nature in situ. "They," wrote a columnist in *Vero Beach Magazine* in 2011, "found their way into the lagoon where, enduring hordes of hungry mosquitoes, they delighted in the swarms of wild birds that rafted the waterway, the timid appearances of clusters of deer, the endless parades of flashing mullet, the silent ballet of dolphins and the slow-moving herds of manatees."

In 1877, an enterprising St. Johns River boat captain, T.J. Lund, managed to bring a small steamboat, the *Pioneer*, through the narrow Haulover Canal that separated the Indian River Lagoon and Mosquito Inlet. Within five

The shallow Indian River Lagoon was opened to commercial boat travel when Captain T.J. Lund brought his small steamer, the *Pioneer*, through the shallow Haulover Canal in 1877. Within five years, approximately two hundred steamboats of all shapes and sizes plied the waterway. *Courtesy of Fred A. Hopwood.*

The *Cleo* was a small steam vessel that worked on the smaller tributaries of the Indian River Lagoon ferrying mail and supplies to small farms and towns along the way. *Courtesy of Fred A. Hopwood.*

years, approximately two hundred steamboats of all shapes and sizes plied the lagoon. The arrival of the steamboats opened the barrier islands that protected the lagoon from the Atlantic Ocean and the mainland to settlement. Along with settlers came townspeople who quickly established small businesses to support the growing population. Small towns became vibrant hubs of commercial activities as skilled craftsmen and merchants provided the services and merchandise needed to support an expanding population. By 1885, the population along the Indian River had grown to an impressive 2,500 persons, and the growth continued.

By the end of the decade, the Indian River Lagoon had become famous for the high quality of citrus fruits and pineapples produced along its shores. Along with the growing number of citrus groves and pineapple fields, small hotels and tourist homes became a critical part of the local economy. Usually ranging from small establishments of five to ten rooms to larger establishments that could accommodate seventy-five to one hundred guests, these hotels did not meet the level of luxury of Henry Flagler's opulent hotels in St. Augustine or Ormond Beach but did provide clean, affordable and comfortable lodgings for America's rising middle class. Guests would often stay for a month or more and frequently come back to the same establishment year after year to enjoy the family atmosphere created by such familiarity. In addition, northern visitors frequently boarded Indian River boats to visit friends and relatives who had settled in the area. The most famous of these was President Grover Cleveland, who, along with his wife, Frances, took the steamboat *Rockledge* to visit his friend Gardner S. Hardee in Rockledge.

The success of the fleet of steamboats on the Indian River lagoon attracted the attention of the railroad baron Henry Flagler, who, having

The *St. Lucie* was one of the large passenger and freight boats operating on a regular schedule on the more than 150-mile-long Indian River Lagoon in the 1880s. *Courtesy of Fred A. Hopwood.*

gained a great deal of fame and business success creating his opulent hotels in St. Augustine, sought to further extend his growing commercial empire southward. The hotels at Rockledge provided small, but continuous, revenue streams, and by 1892, the Flagler system had entered Brevard County. When he was rebuffed in his efforts to purchase existing hotels in the county, he decided to push farther south to present-day Palm Beach. Within a decade, cities like Palm Beach, Boca Raton and Miami had become centers for second homes for the ultra-rich, the rich and the near-rich. Those who did not want to build could stay in the luxury hotels that had become the trademark of Flagler's real estate and transportation network.

With the arrival of the Flagler railroad and hotels came the development of better port facilities to handle the growing number of yachts that ferried the wealthy to these new social centers in Florida. Larger ports were also needed to handle the growing demand for building materials, a trend that would continue in the first two decades of the twentieth century when the boom brought thousands of new residents to the state, each seeking to have a small part of the Florida Dream. They followed the routes established by steamboats and railroads and so, too, would the automobiles that dominated the arrival of new residents in the new century.

Key West, which had been the linchpin in the Union's control of the oceans during the Civil War, continued to maintain its importance in the postwar era. In addition, the system of navigation lights and buoys installed by the federal government as wartime safety measures greatly aided the transit of more and more ships as coastal shipments expanded. Fort Jefferson, once seen as a key defense of the American Gulf Coast, was quietly abandoned with only a caretaker staff. It would remain so until reoccupied and rearmed during the Spanish-American War of 1898.

Just as the East Coast of Florida was booming as steamboats and railroads opened the pathway to the southern portion of the peninsula, so, too, did the Gulf Coast. By the mid-1880s, Fort Myers, Punta Gorda and Boca Grande had experienced explosive growth, fueled by the discovery of phosphate deposits along the Peace River. Tampa, slightly north, also grew somewhat later, spurred by the relocation of cigar production from Key West to that city.

Fort Myers, the site of a Seminole Indian Wars fort and the scene of a minor Civil War battle in 1864, was not a town as such until after the war when, in 1866, a former postman for the Union troops stationed at the fort purchased land there and established a trading post. Ideally located at the mouth of the Caloosahatchee River, its harbor was protected by barrier islands, which made it conducive for shipping. In 1881, Hamilton Disston constructed a canal to link the Caloosahatchee River to Lake Okeechobee, the large freshwater lake in the center of the peninsula. Disston's company also planned to drain the Everglades as part of his projected development of South Florida, a plan that came to naught. The improvements made by Disston made it possible for steamboats to travel the entire seventy miles from the lake to the coast. Many of the steamboats that plied the St. Johns River and the Indian River Lagoon on the Atlantic Coast were eventually put into service on the Caloosahatchee. Cattle destined for Cuban markets, citrus and, most important, phosphate mines in the center of the state used the river and the harbor. By 1885, the town's permanent population had grown to 349 residents, and the town was officially incorporated. That same

Opposite: The *S.V. White* operated primarily as a freighter on the Indian River. Its flat bottom allowed it to dock at the many wharves that were built by citrus growers and pineapple farmers along the shores. *Courtesy of Fred A. Hopwood and Florida Memory*.

Above: Henry Plant followed Henry Flagler's lead and constructed luxury hotels for tourists arriving on his railroad. The famous Tampa Bay Hotel, now home to the University of Tampa, was a favored destination with its minarets, spacious rooms and manicured gardens. *Courtesy of Florida Memory*.

Although most commercial ships had converted to steam power by the end of the 1900s, sailing ships still navigated along the coasts of Florida servicing smaller ports and carrying smaller loads. Some, like the *Florence Harvey*, shown here taking a load of Florida coconuts aboard, later adopted the crude diesel engines to boost their speed. *Courtesy of the Wynne Collection.*

year, the town attracted its most famous resident, Thomas Alva Edison, who, after visiting the area, liked it so much he built a laboratory and a winter home on the banks of the Caloosahatchee.

Punta Gorda and Boca Grande also grew because of the phosphate industry and the easy access to the protected Charlotte Harbor estuary. Extensive loading facilities were erected to offload the many barges that brought the mineral from mines along the Peace River and to transfer it to the larger oceangoing vessels headed for international markets. Phosphate, a natural fertilizer, mined from large deposits in South Carolina and Florida in the 1800s, quickly became the fertilizer of choice for American farmers. So profitable was phosphate mining in the 1880s, land prices along the Peace River rose from $1.25 an acre to over $300.00.

While entrepreneurs were exploiting the phosphate deposits in southwest Florida, tourists were drawn to the area by the abundance of game fish that teemed in the warm Gulf waters. Boca Grande Pass, with its deep natural inlet, soon became a favorite of wealthy British and American sportsmen. By the turn of the century, many of these wealthy elites had built winter homes to take advantage of the moderate weather and fishing. Today, Boca Grande remains an exclusive vacation area for many of the same rich families that first came in the late 1800s.

At the end of the Civil War, Tampa was little more than a rustic fishing village on Tampa Bay. The home to Fort Brooke, a Seminole Wars fort, Tampa had been occupied by Union troops in 1864. Once the war ended, outbreaks of yellow fever and the lack of a sustainable economy resulted in a declining population. With little prospects for improvement, residents voted in 1869 to abolish city government because of the cost involved in maintaining it. When the fort was decommissioned in 1883, Tampa had a population of around five hundred, down from its wartime high of about

Hamilton Disston purchased four million acres of public land in Florida in 1881 and embarked on a failed attempt to drain the Everglades. It was Disston who was responsible for building a canal to connect Lake Okeechobee to the Caloosahatchee River. *Courtesy of the Joe Knetsch Collection.*

one thousand. Within five years, however, Tampa had achieved a dramatic turnaround. The discovery and mining of phosphate in Polk County gave the city's workforce a boost as Tampa joined its sister cities to the south in exporting that valuable commodity. In 1883, Henry Plant's railroad arrived in the city, connecting the city with farms and ranches in the interior. Plant immediately began constructing luxury hotels in the Tampa Bay area that competed with the Flagler hotels on the Atlantic Coast for tourists and winter visitors. In 1885, the city's Board of Trade persuaded Vicente Martinez Ybor, a Key West cigar manufacturer, to move his operations to the area. Ybor came because of the promises of a compliant labor force and because the Tampa harbor allowed for the easy importation of Cuban claro tobacco. The same harbor and the cross-state railroad connections of the Plant System made the shipment of finished cigars fast and easy. By 1900, Tampa had become known as the "Cigar City," as other cigar manufacturers quickly joined Ybor in bringing their operations to the area. Two major settlements, Ybor City and West Tampa, both soon annexed by Tampa, became the centers of cigar production in the world.

The Tampa suburbs of Ybor City and West Tampa became the center of the world's production of fine cigars in the late 1880s and 1890s. *Courtesy of the Florida Historical Society.*

From Tampa north along the Gulf Coast, small villages sprang up, their populations dependent on the plentiful fish in the warm Gulf waters. One of the most unusual was Tarpon Springs, first settled in the mid-1870s. In 1882, Hamilton Disston selected the site for a future city. In 1887, the town became a reality when it became the first incorporated city in present-day Pinellas County. Its future seemed secure when the Orange Belt Railroad, owned by Peter Demens, arrived, but the small town never lived up to its early promise. In the 1880s, John K. Cheney, a local politician and entrepreneur, founded a sponge business. The lure of sponges brought settlers from Key West and the Bahamas to harvest them and send them to markets in northern states. In the 1890s, the city also attracted sponge divers from Greece, and by the turn of the century, the city had taken on the demeanor of a Greek town. It remains so today.

To the north of Tarpon Springs were the Cedar Keys, with a small harbor on Way Key, protected by barrier islands—Atsena Otie Key, Dog

Island, Scale Key and Seahorse Key—that had deep channels between them. First settled in 1843 and used primarily for summer residences by wealthy planters from the mainland, Cedar Keys had a population of 215 in 1860. The completion of the Florida Railroad in 1861 with Fernandina and Cedar Key as its terminals made it a target for the Union navy during the Civil War. In July 1861, a U.S. Navy committee noted that "Cedar Keys affords a reasonably good harbor, though inferior to Charlotte Harbor or Tampa…[but] the connection with Fernandina by railroad gives Cedar Keys its chief importance." By the end of the summer of 1861, Union ships blockaded the area, but the vast open waters and the sanctuary provided by the outlying keys and numerous small islands was enough for blockade runners to evade these warships and conduct a lively trade bringing in arms, ammunition and luxury goods while leaving with cotton, naval stores and tobacco. In February 1862, Union forces, taking advantage of a Confederate troop withdrawal, occupied Cedar Keys and destroyed miles of tracks. Cedar Keys then became a major naval base for the Union.

At the end of the war, Cedar Keys (now collectively referred to as Cedar Key) quickly gained the status of a major port on the Gulf Coast. The railroad had been partially destroyed during the war but was quickly repaired and was fully operational by 1868. The Census of 1870 reported a growing population of four hundred. Cedar Key, the town, which was incorporated in 1869, remained under the control of the Florida Railroad and its subsidiary, the Florida Town Improvement Company, which leased property to prospective settlers on Way Key instead of selling lots.

The immediate postwar picture for the development of Cedar Key looked bright when, in 1865, John Eberhard Faber, a pencil manufacturer, established a mill on Atsena Otie Key opposite the town of Cedar Key to harvest and process the virgin cedar forests that covered the mainland. The Eagle Pencil Company did the same on Way Key. Together the two companies began to ruthlessly decimate the forest while making no effort to replant trees or restore the land. Other, smaller companies joined in, and soon immense tracts of forests in the region gave way to the woodsman's axe. By the early 1880s, as many as two hundred ships lay at anchor in the channels waiting for their cargoes of wood or naval stores. A thriving shipyard was located at Cedar Key, and between 1870 and 1895, twenty-eight wooden-hulled boats were registered from that shipyard. Fishing, oystering and turtling (the corralling and export of green turtles to northern markets) played important secondary roles in Cedar Key's economy.

Confusion reigned on the wharves of Port Tampa as American soldiers prepared to sail to Cuba in 1898. The port of Tampa, while developed enough to handle routine commercial traffic, was not equipped to process the large numbers of soldiers, supplies and artillery that made up the army. *Courtesy of the Tampa Bay History Center.*

At the beginning of the 1880s, Cedar Key was the second-largest city in Florida, yielding the title of "largest" only to Pensacola and far outstripping its nearest rival, Tampa. In 1888, the city could boast a population of over 5,000, while Tampa's was little more than 1,500. By 1890, Tampa's population had grown to 5,532 while Cedar Key's population had started a slow, inexorable decline. After a devastating hurricane in 1896 that wiped out the Eberhard Faber and Eagle Pencil mills, followed by a major fire that destroyed much of the town, Cedar Key settled once again into the role of sleepy fishing village on the Gulf. In its heyday, however, Cedar Key boasted several hotels, restaurants, an opera house and other amenities that made the city a favorite embarkation point for passengers headed for Cuba or Latin America.

What caused the collapse of Cedar Key? One school of thought blamed the decline on Henry Plant's decision to locate the terminus of his railroad system in Tampa after he had been refused the right to purchase land and access to the port in Cedar Key. According to adherents to this idea, Plant had predicted the demise of Cedar Key with a threat, "I'll wipe Cedar Key off the map! Owls will hoot in your attics and hogs will wallow in your deserted streets!" Within ten years, Plant would see his supposed prediction come true. Overharvesting of resources, the effects of a major hurricane

Lieutenant Colonel Theodore Roosevelt, later president, was critical of Tampa's port when he tried to get the men and horses of his Rough Riders aboard the *Concho*, the ship that would take them to Cuba. The majority of the Rough Riders' horses were left in Tampa. *Courtesy of the Joe Knetsch Collection.*

and fire did the job for him. With the end of Cedar Key's reign as a major shipping port, rail service to the island gradually declined until the last train departed on July 7, 1932.

Farther up the Gulf Coast, the prewar ports at St. Marks and Apalachicola dwindled in importance also. Railroads crossing the peninsula and radiating into Georgia and lower Alabama now carried the cotton and tobacco that had once fueled their economies. Like Cedar Key, these small towns now relied on fishing and oystering.

Pensacola, like Key West, remained in Union hands for most of the Civil War. As a result, the city and the port received little in the way of damage and served as a major installation for army and naval forces in the Panhandle. It has remained so ever since. Once the war was over, Pensacola resumed its position as a major port for agricultural products from lower Alabama and Georgia destined for northern markets. In the second half of the nineteenth century, the port at Pensacola also became a transit point for large shipments of iron and steel products from the newly opened mills around Birmingham, Alabama. While much of the iron and steel produced there was shipped by railroads to markets in the North, Pensacola, a mere 250 miles away, proved to be an excellent option to serve markets in Latin and South America.

The post–Civil War period was a time of great economic change for Florida. A steady growth in population and an increasingly important tourist industry opened large portions of the peninsula to settlement. For the 1870s and 1880s, these areas depended on small steam-powered river boats to haul people and supplies, although the expansion of the Flagler System on the east coast and the Plant System on the west coast slowly replaced the reliance on rivers and streams as major arteries of transportation. By 1900, Florida was crisscrossed with railroads connecting all parts of the state. Along the routes of the rails, small towns and villages, once isolated, sprang up to contribute to the evolving economy of Florida. Along the coasts, the pattern was repeated as more and more settlers exploited the aquatic resources offered by the Atlantic and the Gulf of Mexico.

The changes of the latter part of the century, however, would be surpassed in a few decades by the changes wrought by the popularization of the internal combustion engine, the construction of roads and infrastructure and the growth of the use of the automobile.

Inevitable!

7

FLORIDA IN THE NEW CENTURY

1898–1930

*I*mmediately following the short Spanish-American War, when the United States put itself on the international stage, Florida, like much of the old South, was still rural, isolated and feeling its way into the twentieth century. Florida was poor, with a rudimentary transportation system and developing roads and port facilities. Most of North Florida and the central part of the state was still wedded to a system of plantation-style agriculture featuring cotton and tobacco production. Because of sharecropping and peonage, these areas contained most of the state's African American population, controlled by the odious Jim Crow system and among the poorest workers in Florida.

Fernandina, with its naturally deep harbor a beautiful setting, had hardly developed beyond the beginnings of the shrimp fishing industry and some lumber milling. Tampa was still backward and had a population of slightly more than fifteen thousand but was growing as the cigar manufacturing was beginning to hit its stride. Jacksonville, with its growing lumber manufacturing industry and its shipping facilities, had the advantage of being the home of Napoleon Bonaparte Broward and Duncan Upshaw Fletcher, two important political figures in Florida. As a U.S. senator, Fletcher was instrumental in helping the port develop and bringing the navy into the area at Mayport. The fire that nearly destroyed Jacksonville in 1901 brought state militia forces to enforce order in the city, but the rivalry among the various units created their own tensions. The inability of militia units to work together produced a call for a more orderly and organized state military force, which soon became part of the National Guard movement with an annual encampment at Camp Foster at Black Point on the St. Johns.

Elsewhere, Pensacola, which was home to a large naval base, reorganized its facilities to meet the requirements of the navy and improved its ability to handle the region's demand for better transportation. The growth of the timber industry in the Panhandle, coupled with agricultural exports from southern Alabama and Georgia and iron products from Birmingham, had greatly increased the volume of trade from the port, and with this growth in trade came necessary improvements of the port.

The growth did not stop with these well-known and popular ports; the greatest growth was at Key West, which had benefited from military occupation since the 1820s and became a critical staging area during the Spanish-American War. As an entrepôt for cargoes moving through the Caribbean and Gulf of Mexico, Key West flourished. The isolation of the port from the rest of the state ended when Henry Flagler's Florida East Coast Railway (FEC) bridged the water gaps between the many small keys and reached the city in 1912. The arrival of the railroad bolstered the port, however, as plans called for the use of passenger ships and freighters to extend its markets to Cuba and beyond. The Plant System had similar plans for the port.

Flagler's railroad, which extended from Jacksonville to the keys, followed the Atlantic Coast, and as the road pushed south in the 1880s and 1890s, new cities, resorts and ports sprang up. It was the arrival of the FEC that changed Miami from a desolate outpost left over from the Seminole Wars to a modern city, complete with port facilities, up-to-date amenities and intercity transportation networks. It would be Miami and adjacent Miami Beach that would take the leadership role in the great real estate boom of the early 1920s.

The demand for better transportation getting to and from Florida now became an important part of the story. The "good roads" movement of the late 1800s and early 1900s had a tremendous effect on the public perception of the needs in many communities. The development of new technology, like the internal combustion engine, brought a large number of changes to the Florida landscape. The first automobile travelers, the "tin can" tourists, crisscrossed the state exploring every little nook and cranny, and their misadventures negotiating the primitive roads of the peninsula graphically demonstrated the need for better roads.

Led by Governor Napoleon Broward, a movement to reclaim the Everglades for agriculture and development by draining them gained

Following the end of the Great War in 1918, thousands of automobile travelers, known as tin can tourists, came to Florida. Carrying their own lodgings and supplies, they roamed the countryside. A joke of the period said, "They came with ten dollars and an extra pair of underwear, and by the time they left, they had changed neither." *Courtesy of the Florida Historical Society.*

thousands of followers. So, too, did the movement to create a waterways commission, which led to a number of national conventions and meetings where dredging, bridging and reclamation were discussed and widely publicized. Work on the East Coast Intracoastal Canal system connecting Florida with Boston gave a great impetus to this movement. In addition to the railroad systems of Henry Flagler, Henry Plant and William Chipley, the canals and river improvements by the Army Corps of Engineers began to give Florida a different look to potential investors and settlers. The availability of good, reliable transportation was the key to attracting an expanding population between 1900 and 1915.

The years from 1900 to 1915 saw a mini boom in Florida. Revenues from railroad tourism rose a whopping 150 percent. Railway passenger service to Florida peaked in this period and helped create a booming economy, aided by the sales of newly opened land in the southern portion of the state.

European tourists, eager to see the natural wonders of the Sunshine State, also contributed greatly to the economic boom until the outbreak of the world war in 1914 greatly reduced their numbers.

Speculators like Richard Bolles, who purchased 500,000 acres of Florida wetlands and then resold them in small plots to individuals looking for farmlands and investment opportunities, took advantage of the movement of people into South Florida. Many of the plots Bolles sold were still underwater; he promised to drain them but failed to do so. Prosecuted for fraud, Bolles argued that he had believed the hype of the state government about drainage and, with the support of the governor and other state officials, managed to escape punishment. The collapse of the Bolles venture in 1914 hurt the state's economy prior to the outbreak of war in Europe. The scandal associated with Bolles and other unscrupulous scam artists who were also selling underwater plots caused a minor collapse of the land business, as Americans laughed at the audacity of such salesmen and the stupidity of those who bought from them.

Florida's industrial base was still based upon the old frontier industries of forest products, especially lumber. Lumber remained the largest manufacturing sector and accounted for 20 percent of the state's total manufacturing output and about 25 percent of the employment from 1900 until the late 1930s. As William B. Stronge noted, "The lumber industry dominated the state's frontier sector in 1930, as it had in 1900. In fact, lumber increased its share of sector output from 79 percent to 86 percent

Opposite: Mom-and-pop attractions sprang up along Florida roads to provide automobile tourists with entertainment and market Florida products, such as citrus and various craft items. Such operations were the mainstay of the state's tourist economy until the opening of Disney World in 1971. *Courtesy of the Wynne Collection.*

Above: Carl Fisher purchased land on a barrier island near Miami and quickly developed Miami Beach, which, with shrewd marketing, became the hottest properties for sale in the boom of the early 1920s. *Courtesy of the Wynne Collection.*

Fueled by easy credit, the installment plan and lax banking regulations, developers offered speculators the possibility of getting rich quickly by purchasing lots in projected subdivisions. *Courtesy of the Wynne Collection.*

in the 30-year period. The share of both the gum naval stores fell from 10 percent to 7 percent and cattle production fell from 4 percent to 1 percent." The industry produced nearly one billion board feet of lumber per year for almost the entire period from 1900 to 1930.

Traditional southern agricultural industries accounted for only 1 percent of the state's manufacturing output. One of the newer agricultural industries, citrus, grew during this period but still was just recovering from the devastating freezes of the mid-1890s. Florida's cattle industry declined during the first three decades of the twentieth century, primarily because of the loss of the Cuban export market and a trade rivalry with Venezuela and other South American beef exporters.

The outbreak of a cattle tick infestation in the state, which resulted in an embargo on the shipment of cattle to markets, contributed to the decline in cattle exports. In 1923, the Florida legislature passed a law mandating tick eradication. In addition, tastes were changing, and the market's demand for better-fed beef, mostly from corn and grains, greatly reduced the demand for Florida beeves. Florida cattle ranchers still used the open

Florida was very much a southern state during the 1920s, but developers did not want to miss out on sales to the members of the African American middle class, so separate subdivisions and towns were created to attract these buyers and preserve the southern system of Jim Crow. *Courtesy of the Wynne Collection.*

range concept where cattle grazed on native grasses, low in nutrients, that resulted in slaughtered cattle that were tough and stringy, unlike the marbled beef produced from grain feeding. New breeds were introduced in an effort to upgrade the quality of Florida cattle, but many of the new bulls purchased for this purpose died from the tick infestation. The industry stagnated until the early 1930s, when the tick eradication program began to show solid results.

The other major industry of the state, phosphate mining, grew rapidly in the 1880s and 1890s and provided nearly 66 percent of the mining production in the state. Sand, clay, gravel and limestone also provided jobs and income until the First World War. The outbreak of war greatly disrupted the shipping of the industry's output, which brought about a rapid consolidation of the mining operations in the state and eliminated many of the smaller producers. By 1929, fewer than one-third as many operators were in business as there had been in 1900. The state lost many of its markets during and immediately after the war and never regained some of these with the recovery of the 1920s. Yet by 1929, Florida phosphate exports

With the beginning of the boom, Florida promoters developed cutting-edge advertisements that touted the Sunshine State as America's Playground, a concept that still is used today. *Courtesy of the Wynne Collection.*

accounted for about 75 percent of the nation's output by that date and was a significant portion of the world's production.

The First World War brought a number of immediate changes to Florida, and all areas of the state's economy were affected. In southeastern Florida, where the housing boom was just getting started, activities came to a sudden halt. Land development projects slowed when the European war began and came to a screeching halt when the United States entered the war in

Florida cattle suffered from a statewide tick infestation in the 1920s and 1930s that led to an embargo on the sale and export of beeves from the state. As a result, cattle ranching became one of the first victims of the Great Depression. *Courtesy of the Wynne Collection.*

April 1917. Miami historian Arva Parks noted, "Development slowed and in many cases stopped completely. The barely begun Tamiami Trail and the new causeway to Miami Beach were two of the first casualties. Contractors suspended work on the McAllister Hotel and the half-finished Negro Industrial School in Railroad Shops Colored Addition. Young Miamians, including George Merrick, registered for the draft and his brother Charles went off to war." Although some developers tried to finish developments they had already started, they were frustrated by the difficulty in securing enough workers to finish their projects. Dredging projects, like that in Miami's Biscayne Bay, also came to a halt as the Army Corps of Engineers, which had taken over this project in 1916 from the Flagler interests, had to answer the nation's call to wartime duty.

The picture was much the same in many other sections of the state, including the Greater Tampa area, Jacksonville and up and down the eastern coast of Florida. Wayne Flynt, in his study of Duncan Upshaw Fletcher, described the difficulties that faced the citizens of Jacksonville: "Fletcher's Florida constituents suffered heavily. Jacksonville's Schuler Cooperage Company, which exported wrapping paper to Europe, paid freight rates of twenty-three cents per hundred pounds in June 1914. Between August and late October, the company could not obtain shipping at any price…[and by] December the rate had climbed to forty-five cents or an increase of ninety-six percent. This rate drove the company out of the market." In Pensacola, Flynt wrote, "the Chamber of Commerce of Pensacola…complained that firms in that port could not obtain shipping at any price." The Florida citrus industry suffered greatly from the lack of available shipping and the rising costs of insurance, while the lumber business almost disappeared because of the threat of losses to submarines. Edward Keuchel, in his article on the German American Lumber Company, noted that lumber exports dropped greatly with the war along the entire Gulf Coast and that "lumber at the docks was returned to the mills, and vessels ready to sail unloaded their cargoes. Prices on the export market dropped as much as twenty-five percent below the domestic price as European demand decreased fifty-eight percent." The direct effect of the war was immediate and drastic, almost crippling the majority of Florida's few industries.

Once the country became involved in the war, Florida newspapers threw their support wholeheartedly to the effort to defeat the Germans. Anti-German sentiment prevailed in Florida just as it did in most of the country, and the German language, once one of the most popular languages studied next to French, was banned in most Florida school districts. Frankfurters became the ever-popular hot dogs and sauerkraut became "liberty cabbage." In some areas of Florida near the Gulf or Atlantic, rumors of spies, possible invasions and enemy plots were spread regularly. St. Andrews Bay was alleged to be the site of a German plan to build a submarine base, while one couple living near Arcadia even reported that a German neighbor was illegally cutting timber in the area and attempting to smuggle it out, via submarine, on the Peace River.

With the end of the war in November 1918, Floridians were ready to regain the booming economy that had been curtailed during the war. Though hampered by the outbreak of Spanish flu that ravaged the world in 1918, 1919 and 1920 in Miami, Palm Beach, Miami Beach, Boca Raton and Coral Gables, developers like George Merrick, D.P. Davis, Carl Fischer and Addison Mizner began the massive building projects that would ultimately define the state in the first half of the 1920s. Throughout Florida, what was happening along the East Coast was replicated in smaller versions in Tampa, Temple Terrace, Sarasota, Naples and elsewhere. "Wherever there is an acre of land," opined one Floridian, "there is a developer eager to build on it." Lax banking regulations spurred the creation of new banks willing to lend money to developers; nonexistent building codes gave developers a free hand in constructing whatever they wanted to, and a seemingly ever-expanding group of buyers waited for the finished products.

The state's ports and railroads saw a dramatic increase in trade during the boom as essential building materials, speculators, tourists and buyers claimed every available space. Trains coming into Florida were met by the so-called binder boys, real estate salesmen carrying suitcases of deeds to properties that were immediately purchased, resold and sold again—sight unseen! The same scenario was repeated over and over, day after day. So many speculators and buyers came south by railroad during the boom that the rail companies were forced to make a choice between continuing to service their passengers or focus on hauling freight.

As the boom continued, the demand for laborers grew louder and louder. The builders and developers needed labor to complete their projects, while railroads and ports needed manpower to load and unload the steadily increasing volume of building supplies. Labor, however, was in short supply throughout the state, and by early 1926, the boom had slowed dramatically. African Americans, who had traditionally made up the bulk of manual laborers in Florida, departed the state in large numbers immediately after the war. This Great Migration flowed away from the South and into the northern states where jobs in factories paid better wages and educational/political opportunities were greater. There simply were not enough white workers in the state to fill the jobs.

Paul S. George wrote in a 1986 article for the *Florida Historical Quarterly* about the boom in Miami:

> *On August 17, 1925, the Florida East Coast Railway, unable to handle the accumulating mass of building supplies...declared an embargo of all freight coming in carload lots. At the time of the railroad embargo, 851 carloads of freight were parked on Miami sidetracks with another 150 backed up to Lemon City five miles north of the downtown station. Later, the embargo was extended to include...all commodities except foodstuffs.*

Without needed supplies, a collapse of the building boom would certainly happen.

The collapse of the boom came quickly. Three major events sealed the end of the boom. On January 1, 1926, a Danish ship, the *Prins Valdemar*, sank at the mouth of Miami's harbor, blocking ship traffic into and out of the port for several weeks. With the railroad embargo and the closure of the port, even for a limited time, the collapse was inevitable. After the frenzy of the Florida boom in the early 1920s, Florida experienced two devastating hurricanes. The first, in 1926, tore through Miami and South Florida with sustained winds of 150 miles an hour, effectively destroying or wrecking the region's burgeoning building boom and causing an estimated $100 million in damage. The second, in 1928, did the same for the central portion of the state. The dikes surrounding the great Lake Okeechobee, which provided water for the fertile farmlands at the edge of the Everglades, were breached, unleashing floodwaters and drowning an estimated three to five thousand workers and residents.

But not all of Florida benefited during this era of speculation. The rural areas of Florida did not experience huge growth in this period, and wage rates did not meet the national average by substantial margins. Indeed, the relative earnings of Florida workers in the 1920s did not change for the better. As William Stronge noted, "It is clear that the low level of per capita income relative to the national level is the result of low earnings per worker in its industries. It did not reflect a broadly different industry structure." However, Florida was changing, and the number of people employed in agriculture and other extractive industries actually reflected the national trend toward urbanization. The percentage of the population living in rural areas changed from 52 percent in 1900 to 25 percent in 1930.

However, one industry that did thrive in the 1920s and into the 1930s was the commercial fishing industry. This industry was a substantial contributor to the economy in the 1920s and by 1929 was producing about 150,000 pounds on each coast. According to Stronge, the Gulf Coast fisheries brought more per pound than did those on the eastern coast—five cents compared to three cents per pound—and accounted for about two-thirds of the value of the state's fish catch in 1929. The Raffield Fisheries, a major commercial fishing company based in Bay County, became one of the largest firms in the country and was the largest employer on the Gulf Coast. The shrimping industry centered in Fernandina grew rapidly in the 1920s, thanks in part to creative marketing in the Northeast. Mullet was the most valuable of the state's commercial fish in the early 1920s, and the major base for mullet fishermen was in the Cape Sable area of extreme southern Florida. Netting practices among the fisheries began to create shortages in the average catch during the 1920s, and the deputy commissioner of the U.S. Bureau of Fisheries warned against overharvesting—a warning to all concerned about the too efficient netting procedures of some of the older fisheries in Florida.

Florida's other major water-related industry was centered on Tarpon Spring and its annual sponge crop, which approached 400,000 pounds in

Golf, first introduced to Floridians by Colonel J. Hamilton Gillespie in 1904–5, was a mainstay in boom-era advertising. Every major hotel or resort featured a course for visitors. *Courtesy of the Wynne Collection.*

1929. Again, the Bureau of Fisheries warned spongers about the danger of overharvesting the known fields of the sponges. Production reached its peak in 1922, but the value of harvests declined as prices fell—overharvesting resulted in an oversupply. Gradually, the sponge industry faced severe economic problems as overharvesting reduced supplies and experiments with synthetic sponges made from polyurethane proved successful. By the early 1940s, sponging and Tarpon Springs had been reduced to little more than a tourist attraction.

Throughout the boom, tourism in Florida flourished even as the other sectors of the economy failed, making it the second most important part of the state's economy. Tourism accounted for over 70 percent of this sector's contribution to economic growth. By the beginning of the 1920s, when the automobile became affordable for average Americans, the majority of the tourist traffic came via the rapidly developing road network. Most notable was the completion of the Dixie Highway and other offshoots of that route. The creation of the State Road Department in 1915 greatly assisted this development, but most of its impact came after the First World War when the federal government disposed of thousands of surplus motor vehicles used in construction of roads, especially graders, bulldozers and dredging equipment. The *Florida Highways* monthly magazine showed people where the money was being spent, the type of macadamized roads constructed and the locations of tin can tourist camps—popular camping parks—open along the new roads. The magazine also showed the taxpayers of the state how their prison population was put to work building and maintaining the new roads. For many, this so-called reform of the prison system often introduced them to the convict lease system, a system whereby prisoners were leased to private contractors as laborers.

The 1920s in Florida are best remembered for the great land boom and the rapid development of properties in Miami, Fort Lauderdale, Tampa and other places around the state. The decade is also remembered as a period of ever-increasing tourism, the construction of modern roads and the rise of roadside tourist attractions to provide entertainment for the visitors. The United States as a whole experienced tremendous prosperity in the postwar period, and Florida shared that prosperity for a while. However, where other states developed new industries and factories, Florida's major growth was tied to catering to tourists, an economic sector with traditionally lower-paying jobs. This did not bode well for future growth during the 1930s.

8

FLORIDA IN DEPRESSION
AND WAR

1930–1945

*W*hile some historians cite the 1926 hurricane as the start of the Great Depression in the Sunshine State, others maintain that the one in 1928 was the critical blow that ended the prosperity of the early 1920s. Which hurricane had the greater effect is debatable, but what is not debatable is these two natural catastrophes ended the boom of the early 1920s. As a result, the Depression arrived in Florida several years before it became a national one.

Banks, burdened by over-lending and lax regulations, collapsed; planned subdivisions and communities lay dormant in the blazing Florida sun as money became scarce and loans dried up; hotels and resorts, designed to serve the desires of free-spending tourists who no longer came, reduced their staffs or shuttered their doors; farmers, fishermen and livestock ranchers saw their once lucrative markets at home and abroad vanish as the Depression spread rapidly throughout the world; American factories, admired for their efficiency and productivity, shut down or drastically reduced their labor force; and pictures of unemployed workers standing in line for free meals in soup kitchens became the norm. Florida ports, which had experienced their own boom during the heydays of the early 1920s, witnessed a dramatic reduction in the numbers of ship bringing cargoes of building materials and luxury items to the Sunshine State and a corresponding reduction in ships carrying Florida goods to markets that no longer existed. With no money to buy, customers disappeared and trade came to a standstill.

Only Italy and Japan seemed to escape the economic calamity of the Depression. In Italy, dictator Benito Mussolini and the Fascist Party poured massive amounts of government funds into public works projects and into modernizing and expanding the Italian military. Japan, ruled in theory by the emperor but in reality by the military, escaped the Depression because of the tremendous government expenditures that funded its conquests of China, Manchuria and Korea. As Japan expanded its empire, Japanese factories operated overtime to produce the equipment needed by the country's army and navy. To some Americans, these dictatorial governments appeared to hold the keys to rescuing the United States from the economic doldrums, and several Fascist organizations sprang up. Still others looked at the "planned" economy of Soviet Russia and called for a communist-styled government as a solution for the nation's economic troubles.

By 1932, two world leaders had adopted policies and programs that took their origins from all three countries. In Germany, Adolf Hitler, the new chancellor, instituted massive public works programs, improving harbors, building a national network of modern highways and revamping the German military, which had been severely limited by the Treaty of Versailles at the end of World War I. Starting with only a core force of 100,000 soldiers, no armored vehicles and no air force, the military in Germany became the key player in a revived economy, relying on government spending for equipment and personnel, rebuilding the armaments industry and revitalizing other supporting heavy industries. In addition, government construction projects provided work for millions of unemployed Germans and poured much-needed money into the economy. Like Fascist Italy, Germany embraced the concept of a planned economy, and by the mid-1930s, Germany was experiencing a full-scale economic revival.

In the United States, Franklin Delano Roosevelt, who had been elected on his promise to give Americans an economic New Deal, persuaded a reluctant Congress to fund a number of "make work" programs aimed at every segment of the workforce. In order to eliminate older persons from the workforce and theoretically open more jobs for younger workers, the Congress funded the Social Security program, which gave a guaranteed monthly stipend for individuals aged sixty-five or older. From massive construction projects undertaken by the Works Progress Administration to jobs provided for high school and college students through the National Youth Administration, virtually all Americans either participated in an alphabet agency or reaped benefits from their existence. Land confiscation and rehabilitation led to new parks and forests built by the Civilian Conservation Corps, while farmers

The New Deal in Florida focused on efforts to rehabilitate worn-out farmland and provide jobs through "make work" agencies. The Withlacoochee Rehabilitation was one such project. *Courtesy of the Wynne Collection.*

were offered expert advice and assistance from federally funded county agriculture agents. Housewives received information and advice on canning, health, sewing and home management from home demonstration agents, while artists, authors and musicians found employment in various federal programs that sought to expand the cultural horizons of Americans. Some essential industries, such as shipbuilding and steel mills, received subsidies or loans from federal agencies to start new ventures or to revive existing ones and then were offered guaranteed contracts for their products.

Perhaps the most important of the New Deal agencies was the Public Works Administration, an agency that used private companies to construct public works such as schools, hospitals, libraries and other public buildings. Among the projects the PWA funded was the construction of hundreds of municipal airports around the nation. Although not a stated objective of the federal government in funding such projects, many of these airports were built on vast tracts of land that would allow their rapid expansion as training bases if the United States got involved in a war. If they were not needed for military purposes, these airports would become the new "ports" of commerce as Americans readily embraced the potential of the coming Air Age.

African American Floridians experienced the greatest economic difficulties during the Great Depression. Many of the jobs previously reserved for Black laborers were filled by unemployed whites. *Courtesy of the Wynne Collection.*

The 1930s were politically turbulent years for the United States, and Florida was not spared the rise of political extremists. Ybor City, the cigar manufacturing area of Tampa, was home to many Italians, a number of whom identified with Mussolini and the Fascists in Italy. As a result, the pro-Fascist "Silver Shirts" were able to command the fealty of some of these individuals. Some members of the large ethnic German community in Ybor City identified with the Nazi movement. The German American Bund, led by Fritz Kuhn, attracted members from the ranks of that community. Likewise, many ardent Catholics and Protestants were attracted to the antisemitic rhetoric of Father Charles Coughlin, the priest of the Shrine of the Little Flower in Royal Oak, Michigan. This "Radio Priest" spewed his message of hate regularly on radio programs across the nation. Coughlin, once a supporter of Roosevelt and the New Deal, now turned his venom on both. From Louisiana came Huey Long, a radical populist with a program to "Share the Wealth," a call for the confiscation and re-distribution of wealth in the United States. Thrown into the political mix were adherents of Francis E. Townsend's call for a guaranteed minimum subsidy for each

The Works Progress Administration and the Public Works Administration, along with the Civilian Conservation Corps, constructed many municipal airports, which were converted into military training bases during World War II. This is the control tower airport in Vero Beach. It became Vero Beach Naval Air Station in 1942. *Courtesy of the Indian River County Historical Society.*

American each month. Though the field of extremists was crowded, there was still room for a small, but loud, Communist Party, the Ku Klux Klan, southern racists and the ever-present "Yellow Dog" Democrats. Despite the volume of rhetoric espoused by other groups in Florida, the Democrats held the reins of power, and most supported the New Deal and Roosevelt simply because the state was the recipient of millions of dollars in federal funds.

Floridians, like other Americans, watched in horror as German panzers invaded Poland on September 1, 1939. They were even more appalled when England and France, honoring mutual defense pacts, declared war on the Nazi state. Europe found itself in yet another war, and although a declared neutral country, the United States was slowly and inexorably drawn into the conflict.

Within months of the German success in Poland, war came to the Florida coasts as Nazi submarines patrolled the sea lanes close to the shores targeting solitary British ships carrying raw materials. So successful were these submarines, the German submariners referred to the 1940–41 period as "The Happy Times," when they operated freely with little to no opposition from American or British warships. Yet despite the outward appearance of inactivity, things were changing. Florida, always a bulwark for American naval operations in the Atlantic Ocean and the Gulf of Mexico, was slowly preparing for its roles as a major training area and as the first line of defense against German U-boats.

In 1939, three important events occurred that gave the first indications of how critical the state would be to success in the world war that was to come. First, the U.S. Navy dispatched a small team of men to the lonely and desolate barrier island opposite Melbourne on the Indian River Lagoon to begin construction of the Banana River Naval Air Station (BNAS). Located midway between Fernandina to the north and Miami to the south and astride the Gulf Stream, the new base was ideally situated for the implementation of a new form of warfare. No longer wholly dependent on slow-moving warships, BNAS would be home to fast-moving seaplanes that could cover hundreds of miles of open ocean in a matter of hours, bomb enemy submarines and return home safely. With its launching and retrieval ramps safely located on the Indian River Lagoon, BNAS had little to fear from possible enemy attacks short of a full-scale invasion. Aircraft would dominate naval warfare during World War II, as aircraft carriers and airfields replaced battleships and cruisers as the weapons of choice to fight on the open seas.

Second, in 1939, the navy negotiated a deal with the Florida National Guard to purchase Camp Joseph E. Johnston, located at the junction of the St. Johns River and the Ortega River at Black Point, for the purpose of constructing a new naval air station, the Jacksonville Naval Air Station (NAS JAX). The new base, commissioned in October 1940, would become the critical hub for what eventually would become a complex of outlying airfields and training sites during the war. Like BNAS, it also had protected

The Banana River Naval Air Station, constructed in 1939 and 1940, was one of the first new military bases built before the United States entered World War II. It was located on a desolate barrier island along the Indian River Lagoon in Brevard County. *Courtesy of the Wynne Collection.*

ramps for the launching and retrieval of seaplanes. In addition, the navy added three six-thousand-foot runways to accommodate land-based planes. Naval Station Mayport (NSM), located at the mouth of the St. Johns River, was part of the naval complex and was home to a fleet of fast-moving PT boats that could react quickly to submarine attacks. The base also had a runway for airplanes and a protected harbor that was large enough to accommodate aircraft carriers.

The third 1939 event was the purchase of 30,000 acres, gradually increased to 180,000 acres, in rural Clay County for the creation of a new training camp near Starke for the Florida National Guard. This new facility rapidly expanded as an infantry training base and by 1943 was the fourth-largest city in the Sunshine State with 10,000 buildings, the largest hospital facility in the state and the temporary home to more than 800,000 trainees during the years 1941 to 1945. Safely located in the interior of the state, Camp Blanding was impervious to direct enemy attacks.

Government planners surveyed other locations in Florida seeking potential sites for training bases. The state's clear skies and open spaces made it ideal for training new pilots, and private companies in Florida

Above: Naval Station Mayport, located at the mouth of the St. Johns River, was home to a patrol boat (PT boat) training base, and trainees patrolled the coastal waters to prevent German U-boat attacks on passing ships. In addition, sailors regularly patrolled the beaches of North Florida on horseback. *Courtesy of the Wynne Collection.*

Opposite: Construction started on Camp Blanding in 1939. By 1942, it accommodated enough infantry trainees to make it the fourth-largest city in Florida. Its hospital was the largest in the state. By war's end, some 800,000 trainees had passed through its gates. *Courtesy of the Camp Blanding Infantry Museum.*

quickly established schools to train British pilots, as well as Royal Air Force pilots from other nations. American leaders were also preparing for the eventuality of the United States entering the war, and the various municipal airports constructed by the New Deal agencies were subjected to another round of improvements as runways were extended, hangars built and control towers put into place. Military planners divided the Florida peninsula into three areas of control. The U.S. Navy was allocated two zones, with Pensacola the major base for activities in the Gulf, while a string of air stations along the Atlantic Coast were under the command of NAS JAX. The U.S. Army Air Corps/Force was granted control of the central portion of the state along with some areas of the Gulf Coast. By 1945, Florida could count a total of 224 air bases, naval air stations, outlying fields and auxiliary airports under military control. Military

installations of all sizes—from small specialty camps such as the secret radio intercept station at Jupiter to the massive Camp Blanding and Camp Gordon Johnston in Carrabelle—dotted the peninsula, and the skies were filled with every type of plane in the American arsenal from massive bombers to small, nimble fighter planes to cumbersome seaplanes.

Despite the turmoil that had engulfed the world by 1939, merchant ships regularly plied American ports and carried cargo up and down the East and West Coasts. In Florida, citrus growers and truck farmers continued to use American ships to carry their crops to market, and fishermen saw little disruption in sending their harvests to northern consumers. Along the coasts of the United States, lights burned brightly, and Americans luxuriated in the safety provided by massive oceans. Although German U-boats prowled the Atlantic sinking British and French ships, Hitler had decreed that American ships were to be spared, an edict that was rigidly adhered to except for a few instances. As the United States became more involved in supplying war materiel to Great Britain and adopted a policy of armed neutrality, Hitler's order became more and more difficult to obey.

With the conquest of France in June 1940, Americans realized that it was no longer a question of if the United States would become a participant in the war but merely a matter of when the involvement would come. In September 1940, Congress passed the Selective Training and Service Act of 1940, the first peacetime draft in the nation's history, which provided for 900,000 male citizens to be inducted into the armed forces of the United States and serve for a period of one year. The intent of the law was to increase the size of the military and provide a corps of trained soldiers that could be recalled into service if they were needed. Although there were some loud voices protesting the draft as unnecessary and provocative, national polls showed that most Americans supported such a move. The situations in the Far East, where Japan was running rampant in China, and in Europe, where Germany had turned its armed forces against the Low Countries and France, worsened as Italy joined its Nazi and Asian allies in declaring war. Few Americans realistically believed that the United States would escape involvement in what was now a world war, and their fears were realized on December 7, 1941, when the Japanese attacked Pearl Harbor and the United States declared war on Japan on December 8. Nazi Germany and Fascist Italy quickly declared war on the United States.

Realizing how vulnerable the long coastlines of the United States were to enemy attacks, military leaders quickly set up schemes to monitor the coasts for possible intrusions. Armed coastal patrols by U.S. Navy and

The first lines of defense for Floridians before and after the entry of the United States into World War II were the watch towers that were erected along the coast lines manned by volunteers who kept a sharp eye out for German U-boats. *Courtesy of the Wynne Collection.*

Coast Guard personnel were instituted; submarine watch towers, manned by volunteers, were erected along ship routes; and civilian members of the Aircraft Warning Service (AWS), a part of the U.S. Army Ground Observer Corps, kept watch for enemy planes entering American airspace. Seagoing boat owners volunteered their vessels as patrol boats, while aircraft owners and the Civil Air Patrol quickly undertook scheduled flights over ocean waters close to shore to search for U-boats and other hostile crafts. Such diligence paid off. In June 1942, just months after the United States entered the war, two teams of German saboteurs were put ashore by U-boats on Long Island, New York, and at Ponte Vedra Beach, Florida. Although they were quickly captured by the Federal Bureau of Investigation, the so-called Operation Pastorius demonstrated the vulnerability of the extended American coastlines.

Despite the efforts of the American military to safeguard the coasts, it took several months for some Americans to realize that they, too, played an important role in preventing enemy attacks. Following the entry of the United States into World War II, bright lights were visible up and down the coasts as cities and individuals failed to observe the blackout restrictions mandated by military authorities. The failure to do so was brought home to Floridians when, on April 10, 1942, the tanker SS *Gulfamerica* was passing Jacksonville Beach. The amusement park located on the beach had all of its lights on, which silhouetted the ship for a U-boat prowling the sea lanes nearby. Within a few minutes after sighting the ship, the U-boat managed to torpedo it, much to the horror of the people on shore. A month later, the *LaPaz*, a British freighter, was torpedoed off the coast of Cape Canaveral, near the lighthouse on the point. Although *LaPaz* was salvaged, repaired and returned to service, such sinkings demonstrated the need for strictly enforced safety measures along the coasts. Following the sinkings of *Gulfamerica* and *La Paz*, as well as dozens of other ships along Florida coasts, commercial shipping of Florida fruits, vegetables and other products by sea came to an end.

One of the most unusual plans for safeguarding American ships was the 1942 decision by the Roosevelt administration to revive the Cross Florida Barge Canal project. As early as 1567, Pedro Menéndez de Avilés had speculated about the construction of a canal across the peninsula to avoid the long and dangerous trip down the Gulf Stream and around the Keys. The first American interest in such a project came in 1826 when John Calhoun and Daniel Webster petitioned Congress to appropriate funds for a survey of a possible route. Between 1829 and 1911, six more studies

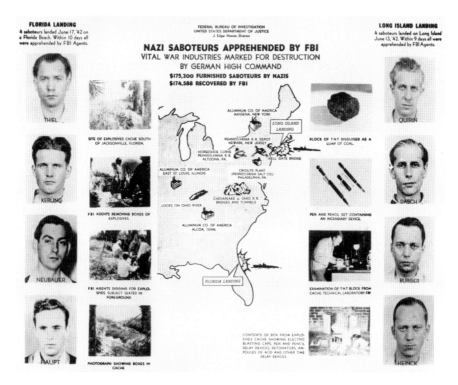

German saboteurs landed on Ponte Vedra Beach in June 1942, and another group of agents landed on Long Island at the same time. The saboteurs were quickly rounded up, convicted by a military tribunal and six of the eight executed within weeks of their arrival. *Courtesy of the Wynne Collection.*

were funded by Congress, and all six rejected the idea as impractical or too expensive. However, in the mid-1930s, the Roosevelt administration, looking for "make work" projects to bolster the economy, latched on to the idea and, in 1935, appropriated $5 million for the project. The project lasted for only three years before the funding ran out, and local protests about damage to the Florida aquifer and national protests over the limited benefits of such a project resulted in Congress refusing to provide more funds. In the early 1940s, when German U-boats threatened ships along Florida's coasts, the idea was revived and touted as a way barges and shallow-draft boats could go safely from the St. Johns River to the Gulf Coast. The war was over before the canal could be completed, but the idea would resurface again in the 1960s before being finally killed for good in 1990.

Other American planners, watching events in Europe and Asia, had been quietly making plans for the eventual entry of the United States into the fray since the mid-1930s. In 1936, after realizing that the American fleet

Merchant ships sailing along Florida coasts did so under the threat of U-boat attacks. The *La Paz* was one victim of a torpedo attack as it passed by Cape Canaveral. The ship was raised and put back into service. *Courtesy of the Wynne Collection.*

of merchant ships was woefully inadequate, Congress passed the Merchant Marine Act, which made funds available to shipyards to construct new ships. The act, which created the United States Maritime Commission, also created the Long Range Shipbuilding Program, which called for the expenditure of funds to construct new shipyards. Sales of steel and iron to industries were curtailed as the federal government reserved those commodities for use in shipbuilding. Following the fall of France in June 1940, the commission sought to create a crash program to construct five hundred merchant ships to replace the British ships sunk by U-boats and to provide the ships that would be necessary should the United States enter the war as an active participant. Planners intended to speed up production by using a common design based on a British model.

Henry J. Kaiser, an American entrepreneur who had gained expertise in the construction business, quickly took advantage of the commission's program and over the course of the next few years opened seven different shipyards. His application of assembly line building techniques, based on those employed in Henry Ford's Detroit factories, dramatically reduced the average time for building a merchant ship from 230 days to three weeks.

Kaiser's methods became the standard for American shipyards, and by 1943, they were producing ships faster than vessels could be destroyed by the German and Japanese navies.

In Florida in 1939, the Tampa Shipbuilding and Engineering Company, which had teetered on the brink of bankruptcy for years, received a loan of $750,000 from the Public Works Administration to build a ten-thousand-ton dry dock. The management of the shipyard was woefully incompetent in meeting deadlines and managing contracts and in 1940 was sold to a group of local businessmen. By war's end, the shipyard, which was known as TASCO or the Tampa Shipbuilding Company, was the city's largest employer, providing work for sixteen thousand men and women recruited from states as far away as Arkansas. During the course of the war, TASCO produced an amazing variety of naval vessels, ranging from the ten-thousand-ton destroyer tenders *Piedmont*, *Sierra* and *Yosemite* to seven ammunition carriers in the *Mazama* and *Mauna Loa* class. In addition to these large supply ships, TASCO also produced twenty-four coastal minesweepers and twelve destroyer escorts, as well as several self-contained barracks barges, repair vessels and smaller cargo ships.

In addition to TASCO, Tampa was home to three other shipyards that produced tugs and smaller ships. Bushnell-Lyons, Tampa Marine and McCloskey's Hooker's Point shipyards operated from 1942 until the end of the war. More than ninety small ships, tugs and tenders were produced by these smaller yards, which also functioned as repair yards for damaged ships or ships that needed refurbishing.

Of the three, perhaps the most interesting was the Hooker's Point yard started by Matthew H. McCloskey Jr., a Philadelphia construction mogul and a powerful Democratic politician. Seeking to avoid delays caused by the scarcity of rolled steel, McCloskey proposed constructing ships out of concrete, a solution that had met with limited success during World War I. To put his plan into operation, McCloskey purchased land on Tampa's ship channel, constructed administrative buildings, built lofts for creating forms and patterns and machine shops, created utility services, paved service roads and erected storage sheds needed to get the operation going. Once again, McCloskey took an unconventional approach in creating his new shipyard, and instead of building construction platforms on dry land, he built three concrete-lined basins, 1,200 feet long, 27 feet deep and 82 feet wide, which were connected to the bay by huge doors. In each basin, three 360-foot-long ships could be built simultaneously. Launching was simply a matter of opening the doors and letting the water in.

This page: TASCO, a Tampa shipyard, was one of several major yards operating in Florida during the war years. At its busiest time, TASCO employed more than sixteen thousand workers. *Courtesy of the Wynne Collection.*

Concrete ships built by the Hooker's Point Yard performed well. Powered by 3,500-horsepower reciprocal engines, the "floating skyscrapers" weathered hurricanes, submarine attacks and hard use. Individuals who served on the concrete ships were most complimentary of their stability, durability and overall seaworthiness. Despite the success of McCloskey's ships, Hooker's Point joined other shipyards in building steel ships using the Kaiser method in 1944. Improved supplies of rolled steel and a shorter production period of ten to fourteen days meant that the three to six weeks needed to produce the smaller concrete ship could not be justified. Although some experiments were undertaken to speed up the "curing" time for the wet concrete, no significant reduction was ever achieved.

Two other Florida cities with large harbors became centers for shipbuilding during World War II. In Jacksonville, the Merrill-Stevens Dry Dock and Repair Company, a local shipbuilding and repair company in business since 1885, entered into a partnership with a New York investment firm to create the St. Johns River Shipbuilding Company, a new company seeking government contracts to build Liberty ships. The new company received an initial investment of $17 million from the United States Maritime Commission and began operations in April 1942. The company produced eighty-two ships during its three years of operation. When it closed in August 1945, the shipyard was the single-largest employer in Duval County, employing a workforce of twenty thousand men and women. Like TASCO in Tampa, the St. Johns company had sent recruiters throughout the southern states looking for laborers, and also like TASCO, it employed African American workers in jobs once thought to be the exclusive domain of privileged white workers.

Jacksonville was an ideal location for a shipyard. The wide and deep St. Johns River provided adequate space to build, launch and anchor ships. Some eighteen miles from the mouth of the St. Johns, the city enjoyed the protection of a naval base at Mayport at the juncture of the river and the ocean as well as the expanding naval base at Black Point. The yard could operate around the clock without having to worry about possible enemy attacks or raids.

There was a second and larger shipyard funded by the Maritime Commission in Florida. In April 1942, the commission selected the J.A. Jones Construction Company, a firm that had been employed building federal housing in Jacksonville, to build a new shipyard for $8.1 million. Within days of signing the initial contract, the Jones Company had selected Panama City as the site of the new yard, filed incorporation papers for a new company—the Panama City Shipbuilding Corporation—opened corporate offices in downtown Panama City and selected a name for the new venture, the Jonathan Wainwright Ship Yard, in honor of General Wainwright, who had been captured by the Japanese when Corregidor Island surrendered in the Philippines.

The initial plan for the Wainwright yard called for the construction of six "ways" to serve as assembly bays prior to launches, some sixty-nine warehouses and specialty buildings and, as the operations got underway, additional buildings for auxiliary services such as lunchrooms and administrative offices. Between 4,500 and 6,000 construction workers were employed in building the shipyard and more than 15,000 workers were employed at its peak production in 1944. Between 1942 and 1945, the yard produced 108 Liberty ships at an average cost of $2 million per ship. The Wainwright Shipyard, nearby Tyndall Army Air Force training base and Eglin Army Air Force Base in Niceville had a dramatic effect on the local economy. Panama City's population exploded from 20,000 residents in 1940 to more than 60,000 by 1945.

The shipyards in Tampa, Jacksonville and Panama City were not the only active shipyards in the Sunshine State. On Lake Beresford, near DeLand, the

The Wainwright Ship Yard in Panama City was constructed in 1942, produced 108 Liberty ships, employed fifteen thousand workers and closed within months of the war's end in 1945. Courtesy of the Bay County Library System.

American Machinery Company produced 29 steel-hulled harbor tugs for the U.S. Army, while in Miami, the Miami Shipbuilding Corporation produced a total of 740 crash boats of various sizes. These boats, which were powered by strong motors, could achieve speeds of 42 knots or better and were used as rescue boats and as fast patrol boats. Perhaps the most unique shipyards of all were those in Dunedin and Lakeland, which produced a military variant of the prewar Roebling Alligator, an amphibious craft originally designed for rescue work following hurricanes in the Everglades. Adopted by the Marine Corps for use as amphibious landing craft, the tracked vehicles also served as lightly armed tanks once the landings were completed. Alligators were also used in the Allied amphibious landings in the European theater.

Florida shores and rivers also served other important purposes. In the Panhandle in Franklin County near Carrabelle, the U.S. Army established a basic training base that encompassed some 160,000 acres of forest and swamp lands. The base, which opened in September 1942, not only provided basic training for soldiers but was also home to specialized training facilities for amphibious units. In addition to the large swath of mainland property, Camp Gordon Johnston also included most of St. George Bay, Alligator

The American Machinery Company on Lake Beresford near DeLand manufactured tugs for use by the U.S. Army in its invasions of the European continent and the Pacific islands. One tug was recently returned and will be open to the public. *Courtesy of the Orange County Regional History Center.*

Above: One of the most unusual marine crafts manufactured in Florida was the Roebling Alligator, an amphibious boat that operated as an armored vehicle on land. It was used by the U.S. Marine Corps and the Army in all theaters of the war. *Courtesy of the University of South Florida Special Collections.*

Left: The need for laborers for American war industries opened many opportunities for women and minorities to move into the mainstream of skilled workers. "Rosie the Riveter," a hit song written in 1943, also became a popular image for women workers in defense factories. *Courtesy of the Wynne Collection.*

Camp Gordon Johnston was a completely new army training base that opened in late 1942 and closed in early 1946. Its primary function was to train operators for amphibious landing crafts, infantry soldiers and soldiers in African American transportation (truck) units. *Courtesy of the Camp Gordon Johnston Museum Carrabelle.*

Bay, Dog Island and St. George Island, where beach assaults were practiced and engineering units learned how to construct temporary ports and docks. Alligator Point was used as a target/bombing range for student pilots at nearby Dale Mabry Army Air Force Base in Tallahassee. From 1942 until the base was closed in early 1946, some ten thousand soldiers were stationed there, although as many as twenty-four thousand could be accommodated for special training exercises. Camp Gordon Johnston was one of three such army amphibious bases in the United States; the other two were located at Camp Edwards, Massachusetts, and Fort Lewis, Washington.

Another unique military training base in Florida was the Underwater Demolition Training base at Fort Pierce, part of the larger Naval Amphibious Training Base Fort Pierce (NATBFP). At more than nineteen thousand acres of land on barrier islands, the base stretched from near Vero Beach southward to Jensen Beach. More than 140,000 naval personnel would receive instruction on the care and handling of various types of landing crafts, such as LSTs, LSMs, LCTs and LCVPs. Divided into two distinct areas, South Beach and North Beach separated by the Fort Pierce Inlet of the Indian River Lagoon, the base was home to a number of different units training for future amphibious landings on the European continent.

The sandy beaches of the South Beach area provided reasonable facsimiles of beaches of Italy or France, and in November 1943, the base became the home of the Joint Army-Navy Experimental Testing Board, an organization that was given the mission of developing and testing techniques and equipment to be used in future joint amphibious landings. Seabee detachments stationed at NATBFP spent their days constructing concrete and steel obstacles—copies of the obstacles found on European beaches—to give the amphibious boat handlers realistic examples of what they would likely encounter in combat situations. Barrage balloon units and naval beach battalions worked in unison perfecting methods for unloading men and equipment under fire and in devising new methods of defending themselves against enemy resistance.

The North Beach area was composed of islands covered by vast expanses of impenetrable wilderness populated by mosquitoes, sandflies and other tropical creatures. North Beach became the exclusive domain of naval combat trainees, including Navy Scouts and Raiders and Naval Combat Demolition Units. The beaches along the Atlantic side of the island provided trainees realistic examples of the kinds of beaches found in the Pacific theater while the opposite shores of the Indian River Lagoon were representative of the riverine environment in the same islands. The Scouts and Raiders were special combat warriors who often went ashore

The Naval Amphibious Training Base Fort Pierce not only trained naval personnel to operate landing craft, but it was also home to the newly formed Underwater Demolition Training Base, the forerunner of today's SEALs. *Courtesy of the Wynne Collection.*

before amphibious landings to scout enemy positions and eliminate them and stayed to direct landing operations. The trainees were required to be in tip-top physical shape, and their training included arduous exercises in running, swimming, obstacle course navigation and hand-to-hand combat. In addition, trainees were expected to master signaling, radio operations, Morse Code and gunnery of all types. Scouts and Raiders received their first combat experience during the American Operation Torch landings in North Africa. After North Africa, the Scouts and Raiders participated in landings in Sicily, Salerno, Anzio, the Adriatic, Normandy and southern France. They also served in the Pacific on a variety of assignments, as Beachmasters and UDTs and even helped train Nationalist Chinese guerrillas for operations against Japanese forces.

The Naval Combat Demolition Units, whose primary task was to destroy underwater obstacles on enemy beaches, gradually morphed into the Underwater Demolition Teams, small teams of men trained in the same manner as Naval Scouts and Raiders but with more emphasized specialties of underwater swimming using a rudimentary breathing apparatus and the use of high explosives. (The UDTs eventually morphed into today's SEALS, highly trained special warfare teams.) Members of the UDTs were men of exceptional physical and mental abilities, but so arduous was the training, the rate of attrition among trainees was 65 to 75 percent. Training for the Scouts and Raiders and the UDTs included the destruction of the underwater obstacles built by the Seabees on South Beach, a continuous cycle of construction and destruction. Along the twenty-five-mile perimeter of NATBFP, civilians living on the opposite shores of the mainland were frequently jolted out of bed as explosions rent the still night air. UDTs trained at the Fort Pierce base were used in both European campaigns and campaigns in the Pacific.

Tourism had always been a significant contributor to the economic well-being of the state, but since the Florida boom of the early 1920s, it had become so important it ranked second behind agriculture in economic importance. Along the coasts, tourist meccas like Miami Beach, St. Augustine and Tampa/Clearwater/St. Petersburg drew millions of visitors each year, and these visitors spent millions of dollars on hotels, sightseeing and aquatic sports. Large luxury hotels, small tourist homes and medium hotels catered to tourists from every economic class, while trailer parks and tourist attractions provided accommodations to those adventurous souls who preferred exploring the Sunshine State in automobiles. With the entry of the United States into World War II, the military immediately took over

Because the Scouts and Raiders and the UDTs used live ordnance in their training and because the area in which they trained was wilderness, it is not uncommon for today's condominium dwellers and developers to occasionally find live explosive devices and ammunition as the barrier islands are cleared for new homes. *Courtesy of the Wynne Collection.*

the larger resort hotels and converted them into training centers, hospitals or recreation centers for military personnel. These existing structures possessed the space for classrooms; the auxiliary services, such as dining and laundry facilities; the communications equipment; and the rooms necessary to immediately begin use as training bases. Miami Beach, the preferred playground of the rich and famous during the 1920s and 1930s, became the location for Air Force Officer Candidate Training schools. Some 140,000 men and women would occupy the luxurious hotels as cadets, and polo fields and beaches became sites for physical training and marching. The storied Ponce de Leon Hotel, and its sister hotels in St. Augustine, became a training site for Coast Guard personnel; beachfront hotels in Daytona Beach were converted into training camps for WAVES and WAACS; the Don Cesar Hotel, a recently completed luxury hotel on St. Petersburg Beach, became a hospital; and so, too, did the world-class Biltmore Hotel in Coral Gables. Even smaller hotels and tourist homes were co-opted for use as lodging for war workers and military families. It was a pattern repeated over and over throughout the state during the war years.

Tourists and military families were encouraged to stay away from visiting Florida in order to keep transportation routes—roads, railroads and rivers—open for military purposes, preserve limited supplies of foods and fuels and keep housing facilities available for war workers. But Americans being Americans, tourists and families largely ignored these government pleas and came anyway. Many came to simply spend time with loved ones who might be facing combat and death soon, others came because they were determined that the war would not disrupt their lifestyles and still others—grifters, gamblers, prostitutes and opportunists—came to take advantage of the lucrative opportunities lonely men and women offered.

World War II changed Florida forever. Of the millions of servicemen and women who trained in the state, many decided to make Florida their home after the war, and the population rose explosively in the postwar years. War workers, recruited from surrounding states, decided to cast their lot with Floridians and remained as permanent citizens. Tourism boomed as hotels and resorts were returned to their prewar owners, while veterans who had

Most of the large resort hotels of Florida, appropriated by the U.S. government to serve as training centers or hospitals, were returned to their owners after the war. The Don Cesar Hotel on St. Petersburg Beach, opened in 1928, was purchased by the army in 1942 for use as a hospital and became a Veterans Administration facility until 1969. *Courtesy of the Wynne Collection.*

trained here brought their families to the Sunshine State to share memories. Small industries, such as oystering and fishing, were quickly brought back to life to supply markets that had suffered from wartime restrictions and rationing. Citrus growers who had been forced to accept limitations on shipping their fruit to markets outside the state found the demand for oranges and grapefruit had not diminished from prewar levels, while the development of orange concentrates made it possible to make citrus products more widely available at a cheaper price and a minimum of waste due to spoilage. Shipyards suffered the most, and what were once mighty engines that powered local economies were closed, greatly downsized or converted to alternative manufacturing sites. Training bases created from municipal airports reverted to local governments, and many flourished as commercial airlines replaced travel on trains and steamers. Even the larger training bases that remained open were reduced in size and personnel as peace ended the need for ultra large standing armies.

Florida and its economy were changed by World War II, but these changes were merely harbingers of larger ones to come in the near future.

9

TOURISM, POPULATION GROWTH, CHANGE AND A TRANSPORTATION REVOLUTION

*W*orld War II was a watershed period for Florida. The United States' military managed to accomplish what entrepreneurs, developers and state agencies had not managed to do in several decades of trying—bringing millions of Americans to the Sunshine State! Although they came as soldiers, they returned in droves after the end of the war as tourists and new residents. Florida's population grew by leaps and bounds during the immediate postwar period, a trend that continues today.

The state's economy, so tightly focused on the war effort for the first half of the 1940s, slowly began to take on its normal prewar status following the end of hostilities. Fishing, shrimping and oystering, severely restricted by wartime regulations and the scarcity of available workers, were rejuvenated as returning veterans and laid-off war workers resumed their peacetime occupations. New markets, fueled by new technologies in refrigeration and transportation, were opened, while older markets, deprived by rationing and restrictions on fuels, eagerly sought to reestablish their claims to Florida's aquatic bounties.

Citrus production, likewise hampered by labor shortages and fuel and fertilizer rationing, quickly resumed full operation. Newly developed canning methods for citrus fruits and juices created fresh outlets for citrus produce, while the wartime innovation of juice concentrates changed the industry's ability to serve only regional and national markets to an international market that spanned the globe. Having a glass of orange or grapefruit juice for breakfast became the norm, as shrewd advertising campaigns sold the idea that citrus products were not only tasty but also healthy. After four years of strict rationing, Americans were ready to indulge in new culinary and taste experiences without limitations, and the connection between indulging and health was too strong to ignore. Florida citrus producers profited from this urge to forsake rationing and partake of new experiences.

So, too, did Florida's truck farmers and fruit growers. Like all areas of the state's economy, farming, whether it was growing corn in Zellwood or strawberries in Plant City or the vast agricultural muck lands in the southern part of the state, had suffered from labor shortages and rationing. When these restrictions were lifted, Florida farmers eagerly resumed full-scale operations. Not all areas of Florida's agricultural economy grew in the immediate postwar period. In the areas of northern Florida that had been tied to the production of cotton and tobacco since the earliest days of territorial Florida, farmers failed to capitalize on the renewed vitality of the postwar recovery. Even before the war, this area had experienced difficult times as the demand for their products, coupled with a mass migration of African American workers from the region to northern cities, had exacerbated the overall effects of the Great Depression. Low wages, social and political repression through the Jim Crow system, outbreaks of violence and the promise of a better life elsewhere in America had caused the migration, and despite some improvements during the war brought about by the policies of the federal government, the once docile and exploitable labor force of Black workers would not return.

Minor industries, such as lumbering and naval stores, fared better as the postwar demand for more affordable housing swept across the United States, but even these industries suffered from the stop-and-go fluctuations of the general economy. Huge swaths of clear-cutting diminished Florida forests in the northern part of the state, and even hasty efforts to replenish the forests through massive tree planting programs were not enough to bring stability to the industries. The minimal time for a yellow pine tree, the dominant tree in southern forests, to mature is twenty to twenty-five years.

What of the massive war industries and military bases created during the war? Shipbuilding, for example, suffered an immediate collapse as the demand for new vessels ended and as surplus ships of all sizes and configurations came on the market. By the end of 1946, the major shipyards in Tampa, Panama City, Jacksonville and Miami had closed their operations or severely reduced their labor forces. Some, like Tampa's TASCO, tried to stay in business by changing their business focus from ships to other products, such as recreation trailers or manufactured housing. It was all

Within months after the end of World War II, army bases and naval stations, hastily constructed to meet the military's needs during the war, were shut down, sold or returned to their original owners. Municipalities took control of military airports and converted them to civilian use. One such base was Hendricks Field in Sebring. *Courtesy of the Wynne Collection.*

for naught, and one by one the large labor pools created by the wartime emergency dissipated. Even the Korean War, which erupted just five years after the end of World War II, did not require the reestablishment of large shipbuilding or aircraft factories because the military could draw whatever it needed from the large reserve fleets and aircraft storage bases that had come into existence by 1946. In Florida, for example, the St. Johns River at Green Cove Springs was considered an ideal venue for one of the largest mothball fleets in the United States, and ships of all kinds—warships, tugs, landing craft and transports—were anchored in neat lines that stretched for miles.

Most of the almost two hundred new military bases created during the war suffered the same fate as the shipyards. By 1946, most of these bases had been deactivated and the properties they occupied either sold back to their original civilian owners or conferred to local municipalities for little or no cost. The massive training base at Camp Blanding shrank from 180,000 acres to a mere 75,000 acres, while Camp Gordon Johnston went from a huge encampment of 165,000 acres to being phased out of operation entirely by early 1946. So, too, were large bases in Fort Myers, Fort Pierce, Melbourne, Lakeland and Tampa, while smaller bases, like those in Orlando, Brooksville, Fort Lauderdale, Daytona, St. Augustine and elsewhere, suffered the same fate. As quickly as these bases had come into existence, they disappeared, remembered mostly by the approximately three million veterans who trained at them and by the local population. It would be these memories that would ultimately fuel the overall recovery of postwar Florida.

FLORIDA POPULATION GROWTH, 1940–2000

Year	Population	Decade Changes
1940	1,897,414	429,203
1950	2,771,305	873,891
1960	4,951,560	2,180,255
1970	6,789,443	1,837,883
1980	9,746,324	2,956,881
1990	12,937,926	3,191,602
2000	15,982,378	3,044,452

U.S. Census Bureau https://fcit.usf.edu/florida/docs/c/census

The growth of modern tourism in the Sunshine State began in the 1920s and reached a prewar peak after Florida's legislature created a special commission to oversee the state's participation in the Century of Progress Fair in Chicago (also known as the Chicago World's Fair). Despite its recognition as creating the most dynamic exhibits at the fair, Florida's efforts, though effective in securing its aims, were soon squashed by the outbreak of world war and by the institution of a strict rationing of essential foods and materials by the federal government. Instead of fun-seeking tourists or permanent residents, the state was flooded by transient military personnel and temporary bases.

No industry grew as much in the immediate postwar period as did Florida tourism. Although tourism had long been a mainstay of the state's economy and although numerous promoters and developers had spent millions of dollars on promoting the peninsula as a paradise over the years, these

Vero Beach Naval Air Station resumed operations as an airport at war's end. It also became the spring training home of the Dodgers professional baseball team. *Courtesy of the Indian River County Historical Society.*

efforts paled when compared to the money spent on attracting visitors in the postwar period—and today. Soldiers who had trained in Florida, out-of-state workers who had labored in war industries, individuals who had seen the exhibits at the 1933 fair and those who were simply filled with a spirit of adventure came to the state in droves. In 1950, Florida counted more than 4.5 million visitors, and by the end of the decade, their numbers had risen to more than 9.0 million. In 1968, less than a decade later, the total number of visitors, as determined by the Florida Department of Commerce, had increased to 20,035,469. The upward trend of annual visitors has continued to the present day. The Florida governor's office placed the number of annual visitors at 117.7 million in 2021, despite the COVID-19 pandemic.

What brought visitors to Florida in the postwar period, and what continues to draw them today? Promoters of the Sunshine State focused on nature as the unique drawing card for tourists. The fact that most American families owned automobiles and that World War II had seen vast improvements and expansions in Florida's system of roads signaled a dramatic change in the way in which tourists came to the Sunshine State. No longer were they confined to the fixed routes of railroads and ships—they were now able to explore the entire state. Mom-and-pop attractions flourished along Florida's roads, touting natural springs, gardens and mini zoos filled with alligators and other creatures from the state's wilderness. Campgrounds, small motor hotels and rooming houses provided lodgings for those who chose to tour the state by automobile. Even before World War II, there were signs, however, that such haphazard operations would soon be a thing of the past.

In 1936, Dick Pope and his wife opened their Cypress Gardens attraction, which featured formal gardens, young ladies elaborately dressed as southern belles and water shows. Marine Studios, now known as Marineland, opened in 1938 and featured trained dolphins and other aquatic creatures as its main attraction. It remains open today. In the immediate postwar period, Newt Perry created the Weeki Wachee Springs attraction, which featured mermaids and underwater ballets. All of these attractions capitalized on the beauty and uniqueness of Florida's flora and fauna.

For those visitors who wanted to experience Florida's wilderness wonders in situ, there was always the Everglades to explore. The Everglades, a vast swamp/river originally encompassing some four thousand square miles, still retained much of its original ecology in the 1940s, although various efforts to drain it had done considerable damage. In 1934, the first national park, designed to protect what remained, was established, and Harry S. Truman formally dedicated it in 1947. Marjory Stoneman Douglas's epic book *The Everglades: River of Grass*, published the same year, brought home to Americans the fragile nature of the Everglades and the urgent need to protect it. By altering or destroying the Everglades, she reasoned, humans were destroying the very foundations of the climate that sustained life in South Florida. With each acre of reclaimed land from the Everglades, the ability of the swamp to collect, filter and store water diminished, and although the national park includes only a portion of the Everglades, it is still an essential part to maintaining a healthy environment for the state. The political and economic battles between ecologists/environmentalists and commercial interests are epic and ongoing in the struggle to find a balance between preserving the natural resources of the state and economic development.

Despite the emphasis on Florida's natural wonders, the tremendous growth in the permanent population and the increasing numbers of annual visitors placed a heavy burden on the state's ecological resources. The opening of Walt Disney World in October 1971 added to the burden on the environment as the theme park attracted 20 million visitors in its first two years of operation, an astonishing statistic then, eclipsed by the

58 million park attendees recorded in 2020. Disney World employed 6,500 workers when it opened its Magic Kingdom theme park in 1971. Currently, Disney World encompasses four theme parks in its thirty-nine-square-mile property, employs 77,000 workers, pays $13 billion in wages each year and operates its own municipal services as the Reedy Creek Independent Tax District. It is Florida's largest employer. The mom-and-pop operations from the past are largely closed, and the smaller attractions like Weeki Wachee, Silver Springs and Cypress Gardens (now the site of Lego Land) struggle to attract visitors.

Although most commercial activities on Florida's rivers and lakes dwindled to almost nothing after World War II, inland waterways continued to be an important part of the state's economy. Slow-moving paddleboats and steamers that once plied the waters were replaced by sleek, fast and luxurious pleasure boats of all sizes. Where local fishermen once sought harvests of mullet and other fish, recreational fishing replaced fishing fleets. Fish houses, citrus and vegetable packing houses built on the edge of the water for ease of access and isolated fishing camps were turned into restaurants, vacation rentals or family camps.

Modern Florida's tourist industry is dependent on the Disney World Theme Park, which draws tourists from around the world to the Sunshine State. First opened in 1971, it is the state's largest employer. *Courtesy of the Post Card Factory.*

Housing for Disney World visitors and workers required land—so, too, did the thousands of workers who came to take jobs with support industries. In addition to Disney, millions of Americans and foreigners bought into the concept of the Sunshine State as an ideal place to live. As a result, thousands of acres of once productive farm, forest and ranch lands were reconfigured to accommodate homes, hotels and apartments for them.

Miami and St. Petersburg, once sarcastically referred to as death's waiting rooms and for retirees only, suddenly took on a new appeal as developers proved determined to put as many people in a confined space as possible. So, too, did other Florida towns and cities, and today condominiums dominate the skyline of virtually every town of any size. The Florida legislature proved amenable to this idea and, in 1963, enacted the Florida Condominium Law, which provided rules for structures owned in common by groups of individuals. A short time later, the legislature enacted rules governing the purchase of time shares, which are similar to condominiums but purchased for a much lower price, guarantee only a week- to two-week period of occupancy each year and can be traded between individuals with time shares in other locations. Coupled with the 1924 state constitutional amendment that prohibited the levying of income and inheritance taxes, the Sunshine State became a magnet for the wealthy, the near wealthy and those on limited retirement incomes.

Following the release of the 1960 film *Where the Boys Are*, Florida also became a magnet for high school and college students seeking new experiences and exploring America's relaxed moral codes. Originally limited to college students, spring break in Florida has become a national trend extending to high school freshmen. So many students come to Florida each spring that several cities, including Fort Lauderdale, have prohibited gatherings, while other cities have reached out to attract them. Such is the tourist industry in the Sunshine State.

Significant changes in modes of transportation came in the postwar years for the Sunshine State. Prior to the 1950s, most visitors to Florida came by steamships or by railroads, but that changed rapidly by the early 1950s, when the majority of tourists began arriving by automobile. Florida roads, like those in most other states, were rudimentary, usually consisting of two lanes and frequently alternating from paved sections of asphalt and brick to dirt roads that were graded by county maintenance crews. In Florida, open range laws meant that cattle and hogs presented dangerous obstacles to automobiles and their passengers since they were allowed to roam freely with no fencing required by law. So frequent were automobile-animal wrecks that those who were dependent on tourism and road transportation demanded change. In 1949, the Florida legislature responded to these demands and enacted a fencing law designed to keep livestock off roads.

By 1950, most Americans relied on automobiles for trips of any distance, and nationally, demands grew for better roads. Dwight D. Eisenhower, elected president in 1952, drew on his experience in World War II and proposed the construction of a national system of interstate highways that would span the United States from the East Coast to the West Coast and from the Canadian border to the tip of Florida. Congress responded in 1956 and passed the Federal Aid Highway Act, a law that provided funding for the construction of new highways and also imposed minimum standards for building them. By 1992, the original system was completed, and the new network provided easy access to virtually every corner of the United States.

A second major change in modes of transportation was also occurring simultaneously with the development of the system of interstate highways, and that was the increasing reliance of travelers on airplanes. Although air travel was not a new mode of travel for Americans, its prewar usage had been limited to wealthier individuals who could afford the expensive tickets. Air travel was also limited to a few larger cities or international locations. World War II brought about another change as Americans became more familiar with airplanes and their overall positive safety record, and the numerous airports used by the military during the war provided convenient landings near smaller cities and towns. Surplus aircraft, no longer needed by the military, flooded the market and were quickly adapted for civilian cargo and passenger service, while rapid technological innovations made air travel even safer and faster. For Florida, these innovations and the availability of airports saw more and more tourists using airplanes as their preferred way to reach the Sunshine State, a mode of travel that has grown annually following the opening of the Disney World theme park in 1971.

Railroads, which had peaked with more than 5,200 miles of track in 1920 during the Florida boom, slowly began to cut passenger service by the 1950s and by 1965 had only 4,500 miles of track in service. Thirty years later, railroads could claim only 2,800 miles of usable track in the Sunshine State. The Florida East Coast Railway gave up its passenger service in 1968 after eight decades, and other rail systems soon followed its lead.

During the immediate postwar years, Florida's ports, once home to steamships from around the globe, experienced a decline in the number of ships each year. Although the number of ships at the ports declined, the volume of traffic increased as ship designs evolved. By the end of the

Drew Field, constructed by the WPA in 1939, became the site of Tampa International Airport at the end of World War II. *Courtesy of the Tony Pizzo Collection, University of South Florida Special Collections.*

1990s, the number of longshoremen employed at the ports also decreased as containers replaced open holds and derricks replaced laborers. Pensacola, Miami, Tampa and Jacksonville became the principal ports in Florida, but smaller ports sought to increase their percentage of trade by undertaking massive improvement projects. Building materials, critical for the expanding markets for new homes, condominiums and apartments for the state's growing population, made up the bulk of the cargoes, but gasoline, foodstuffs and automobiles followed closely behind.

By the late 1960s, smaller ports like Cape Canaveral, Fort Lauderdale, Port Everglades and Tampa expanded their operations with the growing popularity of cruise ships headed for exotic vacation venues in Latin and South America and the Caribbean. What started as a niche market in the late twentieth century became Florida's premier maritime industry by the end of the first decade of the twenty-first century.

Florida's maritime industry underwent tremendous changes during the latter half of the twentieth century, as individuals changed their preferred ways of travel and commerce. As new technologies are developed, as new trends and fashions come into vogue and as new industries are called into existence, more change will take place. Through the changes, maritime activities will persist.

10

FROM THE TWENTIETH CENTURY INTO THE TWENTY-FIRST

*W*ater continues to be a large economic engine in the state of Florida. Florida in the twenty-first century could not continue to grow economically without various sectors based on maritime industries. As the twentieth century ticked off its final years and we moved into the 2000s, maritime industries such as shipping, cruising, fishing and tourism continued to funnel billions of dollars into the state economic engines. These industries employ thousands of people and provide a lifeblood for many families.

The Florida Department of Transportation, Seaport Office (FLDOT) provides a startling look at the economic impact of waterborne commerce. Florida is home to fifteen public seaports, including those dealing with cargo and container shipping, along with cruise lines. The Florida Department of Transportation estimated that in 2016, nearly 900,000 jobs were directly or indirectly supported by maritime industry. More than 107 million tons of cargo passed through the ten container ports located in the state.

Container shipping continues to be a strong industry for the state. Cargo ships arriving and leaving Florida regularly contain fruits, vegetables, fuel, gravel, fertilizer, consumer and manufactured goods and automobiles. Florida is in the top three states in automobile shipments, with the Port of Jacksonville alone accounting for more than 610,000 vehicles moved annually by sixteen different ocean carriers in the year 2021. These automobiles are destined for local delivery, for other ports in the United States and for export to overseas markets.

JaxPort, as the Port of Jacksonville is commonly called, is home to thirty different ocean freight carriers that transport a wide and varied line of products. In addition to automobiles, warehouses on-site allow shipment of consumer goods, forestry products from logs to timber to paper goods, liquefied natural gas and heavy equipment.

JaxPort is one of seventeen United States Strategic Ports as classified by the Department of Defense. From Jacksonville, the military can move cargo for national defense, humanitarian assistance and disaster relief efforts worldwide. The Blount Island Marine Terminal is home to the U.S. Army 832nd Transportation Battalion. Blount Island is strategic due to its prime location. Here, the army is less than nine miles from the St. Johns River, has access to major interstate highways and has direct access to rail service provided by CSX Corporation.

Import and export shipping are strong at the southern end of the state. The chart below shows PortMiami to have experienced tremendous growth in freight that was only moderately slowed by the COVID-19 pandemic and associated economic slowdown. During the period from 2016 until 2021, the total tonnage shipped through PortMiami increased an astounding 45 percent, with the majority of that being inbound tonnage.

CARGO VOLUMES—PORTMIAMI

Item	2016	2017	2018	2019	2020	2021
TEUs*	1,028,156	1,020,192	1,083,586	1,120,913	1,066,738	1,254,062
Cargo Ships Docked	1,231	1,422	1,081	958	868	939
Inbound Tonnage	3,871,906	4,567,926	4,749,255	5,745,632	5,792,134	6,834,613
Outbound Tonnage	3,827,980	4,045,813	4,028,719	4,375,938	3,933,140	4,314,614
Total Tonnage	7,699,886	8,613,739	8,777,974	10,121,570	9,725,274	11,149,227

Source: https://www. miamidade. gov/portmiami/cargo. asp

*Twenty-foot equivalent units—A standard marine shipping container that measures 20 feet long, 8 feet wide and 8.6 feet tall can hold between 9 and 11 pallets in one tier and up to 28 weight tons, subject to ocean carrier's weight limits and applicable axle load limits.

PortMiami demonstrates the global nature of cargo shipping. For the year 2021, PortMiami cargo was valued at more than $76 billion combined inbound and outbound. Scrap metal accounted for the largest dollar volume while fruits and vegetables, a mainstay of the Florida economy, were the fifth largest in dollar volume. Latin America and Caribbean countries are the largest importer and exporter through PortMiami with approximately 52 percent of goods destined for or coming from these countries. Honduras is the largest trade partner through PortMiami, with goods valued at over $11.5 billion. Honduras's main exports to the United States are apparel, electrical machinery, edible fruits and nuts and coffee and tea. In return, the United States ships corn, soybean meal, wheat, pork, wine and beer.

According to the 1980 census, Broward County surpassed the 1 million population threshold for the first time, and by the year 2000 more than 1.6 million residents called the county home. The 2020 population estimate is just under 2 million. Port Everglades, located in Fort Lauderdale, is a significant driver in the economic and population growth of Broward County. As the port is often considered South Florida's "Filling Station," petroleum products, shipped in on huge tankers, were the primary commodity coming through leading into the 1980s. Port officials understood the need to diversify their industry, and by 1980 container traffic was growing quickly. In 1981, the ship MV *Pacific* docked with a cargo of several million pounds of bananas, bringing back the arrival of produce through the port.

The early 1980s saw the construction of rail lines to connect with the port, allowing the Florida East Coast Railway to load and unload freight directly. Additional freight connections were added when the port sold land to the state, allowing for the construction of Interstate 595. Nicknamed the Port Everglades Autobahn, I-595 is an east–west connector to other major highway systems. These enhancements paid dividends quickly, and in 1987 container cargo totaled just under 1.5 million tons.

Military and law enforcement continued their foothold at Port Everglades in 1987 when USS *Leyte Gulf*, a navy ship equipped with *Aegis*-class guided missiles, was commissioned there. It was in the same year that U.S. Customs officials made what at the time was the largest seizure of cocaine on record, more than eight thousand pounds with a then street value of $340 million. An economic impact study determined that navy ship visits contributed an estimated $50 million to the local economy. In a show of respect for the community, the navy deactivated the submarine USS *John C. Calhoun* at Port Everglades, the first ship to be deactivated there. Just three years later, the

USS *Cole*, a guided missile destroyer, was commissioned at a ceremony with five thousand in attendance.

Cargo continues to be an important component of the Port Everglades business model. The Caribbean and Central America comprise 73 percent of imports and 81 percent of TEU exports. As in PortMiami, Honduras is the largest trade partner. The 1990s were growth years for cargo through Port Everglades. More than 23 million tons of freight passed through the port in 1999. Growth in other areas continued as well.

Port Tampa Bay is aggressively seeking out business in the Gulf region of Florida. With a 43-foot-deep channel, almost 500,000 square feet of storage space and easy access to the I-4 corridor, Port Tampa Bay is flexing its muscle in attracting cargo shippers. Bulk cargo facilities are in place for a diverse range of products, including scrap metal, molten sulfur, cement, phosphates, petroleum products, agriculture and more. Port Tampa Bay is also strategically located to take advantage of the growing automobile industry in Mexico. It is forecast that more than five million cars will be imported to the United States from Mexico, allowing for a tremendous growth opportunity with easy highway access for truck pick-up and delivery.

Food and beverage products have a dedicated warehouse space of more than 135,000 square feet with on-site USDA inspections. With Florida having the third-largest population in the United States, the ability to bring food quickly and safely to market has brought Port Tampa Bay to the attention of Publix, Pepsi, Coca-Cola and other large distributors.

Since 2011, the State of Florida has provided more than $1 billion in funding to help assist Florida seaports. This funding has been used to help support a variety of projects. PortMiami has been deepened to fifty feet while JaxPort has been deepened from its original forty-foot depth to forty-seven feet, at a shared cost of more than $420 million. Deepening and widening of channels at other ports have been partially funded as well.

In addition to the direct economic benefits state support has provided for port cities, FLDOT points to the benefits of lessening road congestion as container ships can carry larger loads more efficiently than truck lines. Distribution network improvements have been made, allowing for better rail and highway connectivity to ports throughout the state. The ability to quickly and safely load and unload freight has been improved through the purchase of Post-Panamax Container Cranes.

The Post-Panamax Container Crane is a marvel that modern ports will need in order to remain competitive. Panamax is a term related to size limitations for ships traveling through the Panama Canal. Post-Panamax is related to an increase in ship size allowed due to the newest set of locks at the Panama Canal. With the increase in ship size, an increase in crane size to load and unload ships was needed, thus the Post-Panamax Container Crane. These cranes have the ability to reach across twenty-two containers, allowing for more efficient loading and unloading on larger ships. These electric cranes work on a regenerative power system. While lifting containers they consume power; while lowering containers they create and store power. It is believed that this new system will create savings in not only costs but in emissions as well.

While the cargo industry has been a growing industry, it is not a sexy one. Of the fifteen ports in the Florida Seaport System, six support cruise lines. It is the cruise industry that garners a large portion of the news when it comes to the maritime industry in Florida. And that is not unjustifiable.

In studying the economic history of Florida, economist William B. Stronge discovered that the cruise industry did not explode in the state until after 1960. In 1960, Stronge found that the passenger head count was only 300,000. This number grew slowly, but steadily, and in 1975 it was around 700,000 before rocketing to 1.4 million in 1980.

Port Canaveral has grown from a small fishing port and submarine base into a full-fledged cruise port with seven different ships making scheduled departures and arrivals. In addition, Port Canaveral has developed its cargo loading and unloading facilities in an effort to attract more commercial traffic. *Courtesy of the Post Card Factory*.

This passenger growth continued strong through the last two decades of the twentieth century, reaching almost seven million passengers by the year 2000. In that year, Florida accounted for almost 50 percent of all cruise travel embarkments in the United States. Much of this growth is accounted for by the increased availability and affordability of commercial flight. Passengers became better able to reach and depart their port, allowing them to spend more of their vacation on the water, rather than in transit. By 1980, three ports were already dominant in the industry: PortMiami, Port Canaveral and Port Everglades. These three have continued to prove most popular with visitors. With large and convenient airports nearby, East Coast ports and their proximity to the popular Caribbean cruise destinations continue to be a favorite of cruise travelers.

In 2019, before the impact of the COVID-19 pandemic, cruising from Florida continued to be a popular vacation idea. The Florida Cruise Industry Economic Impact Report for 2019 states that 8.29 million passengers, 2.3 million of them Floridians, embarked on a cruise from Florida, providing $9.04 billion in direct spending, and supported almost 160,000 jobs. Further, Carnival, Disney Cruise Line, MSC Cruises, Norwegian Cruise Line and Royal Caribbean International all maintain headquarters in the state. In the post-pandemic world, the popularity of cruising does not seem to have faltered. Cruise Industry News reported in January 2022 that the three largest ports in Florida will be home soon to an estimated fifty-five ships containing almost 160,000 berths.

PortMiami leads the way with twenty-five ships docking there, containing over sixty-seven thousand berths. Port Everglades has twenty ships operating from their docks containing over fifty-five thousand berths, while Port Canaveral is home to thirteen ships and more than forty thousand berths. While Port Canaveral may seem small with only thirteen ships, it is the second-busiest port for multiday embarkations, and it is home to the important Disney *Dream*, Disney *Fantasy* and the brand-new Disney *Wish* ships. These themed ships offer cruises tied to vacations at the Walt Disney World Resort, further fueling the Florida economy.

Cruise ships were a primary cause of concern during the early days of the COVID-19 pandemic. Thousands of people grouped together in tight quarters made for potentially dangerous times. Despite increased vaccination levels and additional precautions taken by the industry, COVID cases still occur on cruise ships, though at a much lower level than previously. Despite potential risks, vacationers flocked back to cruise ships and continue to do so. Port Canaveral projected more than $150 million in revenue for the fiscal year beginning on October 1, 2022. The port anticipates using much of the profits to enhance existing facilities. Port Canaveral is anticipating continued growth with the addition of new ships and a new cruise line, Marella, docking on-site. Compared with 2019, the number of cabins available has increased a staggering 32 percent. These cabins are being booked, and demand continues strong. In the week of July 8 through 14, 2022, more than 107,000 passengers were welcomed through Port Canaveral, the largest weekly total since the port opened to cruise traffic in 1964.

PortMiami continues to live up to its nickname of the "Cruise Capital of the World." MSC Cruises and the City of Miami broke ground in March 2022 on a new terminal that will be able to accommodate up to thirty-six thousand passengers per day when complete in 2023. This will be the largest cruise terminal in North America. In February 2022, Virgin Voyages unveiled Terminal V at PortMiami. Sir Richard Branson's new cruise line will call Miami home with ships departing to the Caribbean, including a stop at a Virgin-owned club in Bimini. While celebrating the new with Virgin Voyages, PortMiami also recently celebrated a fiftieth anniversary with Carnival Cruise Lines. In 1972, Carnival launched its first ship, the TSS *Mardi Gras*, from PortMiami.

Economist William B. Stronge pointed out the economic diversity provided by the cruise industry, "Since cruise ships are essentially large hotel resorts that happen to float on the sea, they have similar impacts on the state economy." The industry must purchase the tons of supplies needed to fulfill the needs of thousands of cruisers. This includes food and dining supplies, towels and other toiletries, cleaners and more. Large numbers of employees are locally sourced, including chefs, wait staff, housekeeping, hospitality, entertainers, dock workers and a multitude of land-based support staff. Ship maintenance is often handled in Florida. Cruise line companies pay port fees and property taxes that help support local counties. Stronge reported that in 2000, Florida received more than one-third of all cruise industry expenditures in the United States.

In addition to the multiday cruise industry, the single-day gambling cruise industry continues to be robust, though on a smaller scale than in prior years. Online gambling and legal gambling at casinos on Native American lands have slashed the number of day gambling cruises. Victory Casino Cruises operates Las Vegas–based casino-style cruises based out of Port Canaveral. These ships depart the port and leave Florida waters before offering table games and slot machines. Entertainment and food are provided in addition to gambling.

While the cruise industry would seem to lack controversy and brings a large increase in economic activity to associated ports, that is not always the case, and the residents of Key West have fought back against the industry. The cruise industry can trace its Key West roots to 1969, when the *Sunward* docked at the Port of Key West. The ship docked approximately once each month. By the early 1970s, the cruise ship *Bolero* was making weekly stops. During the 1980s, the city made improvements to the Mallory Dock, turning it into a full cruise ship docking facility. By fiscal year 1992–93, approximately 256,000 cruise passengers visited Key West, a number that grew exponentially to 1,122,200 over the next decade. In 2019, it is estimated that nearly 1 million passengers visited the island community because of cruise ships.

As the number of ships, passengers and the size of ships has increased, residents of Key West have voiced concerns of the impact to the small island community. Residents created the organization Key West Committee for Safer Cleaner Ships, a not-for-profit group committed to limiting the size of ships and number of cruise-related visitors to the island. Their goal is to "balance the limited economic benefits of cruise ships against the larger public health, environmental, and economic interests of Key West citizens."

At the backbone of this movement is the Murray Report, a 2005 study on the effect of the cruise industry on Key West. Thomas J. Murray & Associates reported chronic water quality issues, an assessment that was upheld by Dr. Henry Briceno of the Florida International University Institute of Environmental Water Quality Monitoring Lab during the cruise ship shutdown associated with COVID-19. Turbidity, the cloudy appearance of water, decreased and the amount of dissolved oxygen increased, both signs of a healthier water system. While these data are preliminary, they do point to a potential long-term disturbance due to large cruise vessels. The Murray Report further concluded that large ships had a negative impact on coral reefs and negatively affected conch and lobster populations. Cruises were said to have a negative effect on the commercial and charter fishing industries as well.

The economic impact of cruise visitors to Key West is in dispute, as might be expected. The pro–cruise industry voices tout that cruise visitors spend an average of approximately $9.34 per hour, while overnight visitors spend $6.34 per hour. The per hour figure is highly misleading, as overnight visitors spend roughly one-third of their visit sleeping.

The cruise industry reported that in 2019, Key West had an unemployment rate of 2.0 percent and the industry accounted for the equivalent of eight hundred jobs. They claim that eliminating cruise visitors would cause an unemployment jump to 6.5 percent. They concluded their report by stating, "The economic contribution of cruise visitors aids in the development of the flourishing economic ecosystem [an interesting choice of words] by providing substantial inflows for the food and beverage, retail, and recreation sectors and supporting nearly 1-in-20 jobs in the city."

In the November 2020 election, voters in Key West approved three referenda changing how the cruise industry could operate there. The first prohibited cruise ships of more than 1,300 passengers from docking in the Keys. The second placed a limit of 1,500 cruise ship visitors daily to the island. A final measure mandated priority docking to cruise lines with the best environmental and health records.

In barely six months' time, Florida governor Ron DeSantis and Republican lawmakers, backed by industry campaign contributions, passed and signed into law CS/CS/Cs/SB 1194 (2021) Transportation Bill, including the following provision:

> *Notwithstanding any other law to the contrary, a local government may not restrict or regulate commerce in the seaports of this state, as listed in s.311.09, including, but not limited to, regulating, or restricting a vessel's type or size, source or type of cargo, or number, origin, or nationality of passengers. All such matters are expressly preempted to the state.*

Key West officials have not given up the fight, however, and, in March 2022, passed a resolution directing cruise traffic away from the city-owned Mallory Dock and the Outer Mole Pier. This resolution directed cruise traffic to the privately owned Pier B to "ensure that cruise ship activity at the Pier B dock and any private property conforms to state and federal regulations." This resolution is under state review with the outcome uncertain.

Florida tourism is dependent on water in ways other than the cruise industry. Visit Florida reports that Florida enjoyed more than 131 million visitors in 2019 (the last year prior to the COVID-19 pandemic). Not all these visitors ended up in Orlando at theme parks. Visitors come to Florida to enjoy the beaches. Volusia County, home to Daytona Beach, "the World's Most Famous Beach," welcomed 10 million visitors in 2019 with an economic impact of $6.2 billion. Florida state parks are often directly tied to water. Some of the most popular include Blue Spring State Park, famed as a winter retreat for manatee populations; snorkeling and diving at John Pennekamp Coral Reef State Park; and, for the more adventurous, the Florida Circumnavigational Saltwater Paddling Trail, a more than 1,500-

Tourists who come to Florida are drawn to the state's exotic wildlife and aquatic creatures. Manatees, dolphins and wild birds are among the favorite attractions. *Courtesy of the Post Card Factory*.

mile water trail featuring twenty-six stops allowing paddlers to travel from one side of the state to the other.

Museums are another key component in sharing the importance of maritime history and industries in Florida. Organizations across the state are eager to collect, preserve and share various aspects of Florida's maritime history. In Gainesville, the Florida Museum of Natural History is adding a new exhibit to its already stellar lineup. The exhibit, *The Story of Florida Water*, proposes to tell the past, present and future of water in Florida. In Walton County, visitors can view the Underwater Museum of Art, located in the Gulf of Mexico. Located almost one mile from shore, at a depth of fifty-eight feet, this ecotourism attraction draws visitors, divers and marine life to its ever-expanding exhibits. The Jacksonville Naval Museum seeks to operate the USS *Orleck* as the "US Navy Cold War Experience," while the DeLand Historical Trust is hoping to find a location for, and ultimately rehabilitate, a World War II–era tugboat, the *ST479*, built in DeLand, that might have served during the Normandy invasion. This tugboat, once on exhibit, will help tie Florida manufacturing and homefront efforts to the larger story of World War II.

Florida's role in World War II continues to fascinate residents and tourists, as witnessed by the numerous small museums created to celebrate that heritage. Among the little-known but important contributions made by Floridians were those made by workers at the American Machinery Company at Lake Beresford who manufactured harbor tugs for the army. *Courtesy of the Orange County Regional History Center.*

At the Florida Maritime Museum in Cortez, visitors will see a collection of artifacts that help tell the story of Florida's fishing and maritime past from Native cultures through today's modern large-scale commercial fisheries. In 2025, the Gulf Coast Maritime Museum in Sarasota will open a facility dedicated to the history of boat building on the Gulf Coast of Florida. The Mel Fisher Maritime Museum in Key West has been organized to "research, interpret, and exhibit the maritime history of Florida and the Caribbean in ways that increase knowledge, enrich the spirit, and stimulate inquiry." National Park Service sites such as the Castillo de San Marcos in St. Augustine and Fort Matanzas, just to its south, highlight the key roles played by the ocean and inlets during the formative years of the state.

Lighthouses all along the coastline of Florida hold fascination for visitors. Many are open to the public with artifacts and interpretive exhibits. While the hard life of a lighthouse keeper is in the past, several of these beacons are available for climbing, allowing visitors a slight glimpse into what it might have been like to serve as a principal keeper or as an assistant keeper. Perhaps the most well known are the St. Augustine Light Station and the Ponce de Leon Inlet Light Station. Both stations have active lights and are open to the public.

Theme parks have not lost sight of the value of water. Locations such as Gatorland, the Miami Seaquarium, Weekie Wachee Springs State Park and Silver Springs State Park harken back to the days of the roadside attraction. These attractions are now often niche in nature but fill an important role. They provide educational opportunities along with entertainment at prices considerably less than large theme parks. Where can you see a live mermaid show other than Weekie Wachee?

The large theme parks have not ignored the appeal of water-based attractions. The most prominent is Sea World. While often derided for its animal training and shows, Sea World plays an important role in sea animal rehabilitation while educating and entertaining millions of visitors. Walt Disney World Resort offers visitors Typhoon Lagoon and Disney's Blizzard Beach, while Universal Studios offers thrills at Volcano Bay. While

Small roadside attractions and fruit stands still receive a share of Florida's annual tourist visitors, but that share is slowly diminishing because many of them are located along less traveled roads and in smaller towns that cannot compete with the interstate highways and multiple attractions in urban areas. *Courtesy of the Post Card Factory.*

not Florida themed, the Walt Disney World Magic Kingdom is home to the extremely popular Pirates of the Caribbean, Jungle Cruise and the Liberty Square Riverboat. To get to the Magic Kingdom, guests can ride one of the iconic ferryboats.

Surfing has a long history in Florida dating back to the 1930s. Today, New Smyrna Beach and Cocoa Beach are often considered the leading surf spots in the state. New Smyrna Beach is affectionately called the "Shark Bite Capital of the World" even though you are more likely to be struck by lightning than be bitten by a shark. In 2019, there were 28 shark bites registered in the state of Florida, with Volusia County recording 17 of these. The world total of alleged shark bites for 2019 was only 137. Today, surf history is kept alive at museums such as the Florida Surf Museum in Cocoa Beach and an exhibit, donated by the Museum of East Coast Surfing New Smyrna Beach, located within the New Smyrna Museum of History. Other key players in promoting the history of Florida surfing include the Palm Beach County Surfing History Project, the St. Augustine Surf Culture and History Museum, the Smyrna Surfari Club and the Florida Surf Film Festival, which features some of the biggest names in documentary surf films, hosting events in New Smyrna Beach.

Household names such as Ron Jon and Hawaiian Tropic can trace their origins to Florida. While Ron Jon Surf Shop first opened in Long Island Beach, New Jersey, in 1961, founder Ron DiMenna had relocated to Cocoa Beach by 1963, opening his iconic Ron Jon Surf Shop, a brand that thrives in multiple locations throughout the country and on the bumpers of thousands of cars. Ron Rice started Hawaiian Tropic in 1969 with a $500 loan before selling the sun protection brand to Playtex in 2007 in a deal valued at $83 million.

In addition to the cargo, tourism and cruise industries, the seafood and aquaculture industries are an important part of the maritime history of Florida. The Florida Department of Agriculture and Consumer Services reports that Florida ranked eleventh nationally in 2016, with more than 87 million pounds of seafood harvested at a value of more than $237 million. The Florida Fish and Wildlife Conservation Commission (FFWCC) reports 1.5 million saltwater fishing licenses were sold in fiscal year 2019–20 and that there were nearly 2.5 million active licenses during that time frame. The FFWCC states that the economic impact of salt- and freshwater fishing combined is just under $14 billion and supports 120,000 jobs.

While commercial fishing continues to be a successful industry, there are concerns that overfishing may be occurring. Florida International

University (FIU) simply defines overfishing as "when people [commercial or recreational anglers] reduce a population by catching too much." FIU states that overfishing is not only an environmental and ecosystem issue but also grows larger when it creates a food crisis and potential loss of employment for those in the industry. The National Oceanic and Atmospheric Administration (NOAA) has identified grouper and snapper as two species highly vulnerable to overfishing.

FIU professor Alastair Harborne has explained how overfishing affects not only one species: "Overfishing can have a range of impacts on the environment because it upsets the delicate balance of marine food webs. If one species is overexploited, it can have cascading effects on lots of other species." Dr. Harborne adds, "Furthermore, fish have an important role in marine ecosystems. For example, parrotfish on coral reefs eat seaweed and allow corals to flourish. If fish such as parrotfish are overfished, they cannot carry out these roles."

One of the primary responses to the concern of overfishing is the sustainability movement. The Marine Stewardship Council defines sustainable fishing as "leaving enough fish in the ocean and protecting habitats and threatened species. By safeguarding the oceans, people who depend on fishing can maintain their livelihoods." The Nature Conservancy puts some meat on these bones in discussing the term *fisheries management*. Fisheries management is the mix of fishing guidelines and practices that prevent fish from being harvested in an unsustainable manner. Proper fisheries management does not just lay down laws but involves anglers, showing them where they can fish, the tackle that can be used and size restrictions and teaching them the value of what scientists are seeking to accomplish. By partnering with those whose livelihood may be on the line, fish stocks can be preserved for generations to come.

No discussion of the modern maritime history of Florida is complete without a discussion of sea level rise. The University of California Museum of Paleontology (UCMOP) describes several factors believed to be affecting sea levels today. The first are human activities, including the burning of fossil fuels, deforestation and agricultural activities. These human activities are helping lead to an increase in average global temperatures, which in turn cause a melting of glaciers and ice caps. As liquid water absorbs heat from the atmosphere it expands, causing it to take more space, a phenomenon called thermal expansion.

Two earth system processes are also leading to sea level rise. Tectonic activity, which in simplistic terms is the uplifting or sinking of land at a particular location, can affect localized sea levels through the distribution, size and depth of ocean basins. Ocean circulation patterns, the natural method of how water is distributed, can also cause sea levels to rise in certain locations. UCMOP states that sea level rise between 1993 and 2015 was roughly seventy millimeters, or approximately two and three-quarters of an inch. While this may seem like a very small rise, a key factor to remember is that sea level rise is not consistent throughout the globe.

Sea level rise, and the response to it, is often dependent on local factors. The South Florida peninsula is an area that appears to have the potential to be heavily affected by sea level rise. The area is at a low elevation; Miami is roughly six feet above sea level, with an extremely flat topography. Scientists writing in the *Journal of Marine Science and Engineering* say these two factors create an ideal setting for sea level rise and potential flooding.

The rise of sea levels is more than just a concern over displacing persons and their physical structures. Saltwater intrusion can have a direct effect on freshwater quality and availability. A decrease in freshwater supply, coupled with increased demand from population growth in the area, is a combination that will be difficult for governmental planners to solve.

Joseph Park proposed that by the year 2075, sea level rise could increase by as much as ninety-one centimeters, nearly thirty-six inches, a level at which marine conditions could intrude on areas of the Everglades and other freshwater marshes. At these levels, an increase in tidal flooding can be expected and a decrease in ability to discharge these floodwaters will be standard.

Miami-Dade County has highlighted several concerns related to sea level rise, including increased storm surge, canal and tidal flooding, higher groundwater levels, saltwater intrusion, increased wave heights and shoreline erosion. These direct concerns will affect residents through increased risks that lead to increased costs in homeownership and rents. Transportation concerns such as road and bridge flooding and washout will become more common. These increased costs will disproportionately affect already marginalized populations such as the homeless, those with limited English skills, the elderly and rural populations.

Several solutions are already being implemented by Miami-Dade County. Expanding education on flood risk is crucial. With the multicultural population of South Florida, this is being done in multiple languages to reach as many residents as possible. Science-based education is being distributed through the school system, libraries, governments and public assistance programs.

Climate change, diminishing freshwater sources and pollution are major concerns for Floridians. Scientists predict that the fabled Florida beaches and the Everglades will be submerged by rises in the sea level as early as 2050. The question then arises—What happens to the state's economy and population growth? *Courtesy of the Post Card Factory*.

The need to elevate existing structures, equipment and roads is being evaluated along with the need to elevate new construction. Improvements must be undertaken in stormwater management, including increased drainage and improved pumping abilities. Close cooperation with the South Florida Water Management District will be crucial in achieving this goal. Communities need to consider expanding greenways in higher-risk areas. This might include offering to purchase properties from owners who have been flooded multiple times. Educating property owners on the need for flood insurance is ongoing. With a rising percentage of damage being the result of floodwaters, traditional insurance may not cover these damages.

Maintaining freshwater supplies is crucial if saltwater intrusion is to occur. Property owners will need to address septic systems to make them less susceptible to rising groundwater levels. Cities must address maintenance issues related to water and sewage pipes and manholes to prevent saltwater intrusion. By slowing the movement of saltwater through local canal systems, wetland areas can be restored. Mangroves will then be able to rejuvenate, which will further slow saltwater movement.

Finally, allowing nature to work on its own is crucial. Restoration of the Everglades will go a long way in maintaining freshwater supplies. This will take the input of the federal government, as the cost to reestablish the natural water flow through these lands would be cost-prohibitive for local agencies. Restoring the Everglades has other benefits as well. Natural habitats for fish, birds, alligators, manatees and more will be restored. This will in turn pay economic dividends as the real estate, fishing and tourism industries flourish.

The maritime industry is vital to the continued growth and future success of Florida. While much of Florida's past is based on the exploitation of water, residents will continue to rely on the ocean, rivers and lakes of the Sunshine State for both industry and personal enjoyment. Millions of residents depend either directly or indirectly on the success of our waterways. Fishing, shipping and tourism rely on a healthy marine environment for their success. As the twenty-first century progresses, maritime concerns will continue to be at the forefront of political and economic discussions.

EPILOGUE

When Juan Ponce de Leon and the Spanish discovered La Florida by way of water, they could never have imagined the lands being home to nearly twenty-two million people. With water surrounding three sides of the state—the Gulf of Mexico to the west, the Atlantic Ocean to the east and the Straits of Florida to the south— Florida, then, as now, is dependent on water. From its earliest days through the present, the issue of water has been dominant in the minds of many Floridians. Whether it be economics, military matters, sports, drinking or conservation, water is truly vital for every aspect of Florida.

The use of waterways has played a crucial role in the development of Florida, from what was once a small, lightly populated territory, to what is now the third-most populous state in the Union. Long before Europeans set foot in Florida, Native Americans were using dugout canoes to navigate riverways carrying both people and goods. As Florida changed ownership due to the shifting fates of war, water played a vital role. Cartographers created maps, allowing for a more precise idea of Florida geography. Agricultural and forest industries dominated the Florida economy, and their harvests were shipped to markets around the world.

During the nineteenth century, the military exploited Florida's waterways. The U.S. Navy understood the importance of Key West as a base. In addition to the revenue brought in by the military, Key West also profited from small industries that sprang up. Soon, the small, isolated port became one of the wealthiest cities in the United States.

The issue of slavery fueled the secession of Florida from the Union during the lead up to the American Civil War. Water played a vital role when the Union attempted to institute a naval blockade to prevent goods from leaving or entering Confederate ports and inlets. Blockade runners were vital in moving crops to market and bringing in needed supplies for Florida residents. In the post–Civil War years, the population of Florida began to steadily grow. In addition to crops, the tourism industry emerged. Rivers became highways, providing tourists a convenient way to travel into the Florida heartland.

In the twentieth century, economic booms and the expansion of the U.S. military continued to show the importance of maritime activities in Florida. Commercial fishing, tourism and land development fueled economic growth after World War I but could not stave off the onset of the Depression. In World War II, Florida played a key role in training soldiers in preparation for America's involvement. Shipbuilding and repair became vital industries. Women were thrust into the workforce, a status they were reluctant to abandon. Waterfront cities such as Tampa, Jacksonville, Miami and Panama City, along with smaller towns, played key roles in shipbuilding. Training facilities, large and small, were located throughout the state.

In the postwar years, soldiers and their families returned to Florida by the millions—some as visitors and some as permanent residents. While war-related industries declined, tourism expanded. Automobile ownership allowed a family to cram into their sedan and head to attractions such as Marineland, Weeki Wachee or a host of alligator farms.

Today, water continues to be a major focus for Florida's population as the growth in residents has strained resources. Municipalities are faced with increased needs for water, and the Environmental Protection Agency estimates that by 2030 Florida's need for fresh water will have increased 28 percent over that of 2005. Planners have worked hard to mitigate this impact where possible. Lawn watering restrictions and the use of reclaimed water are now in place in most communities. Low-flow toilets and improved shower technology are the norm in new construction projects and are crucial in reducing residential water usage. Florida's economic dependence on water, while changing, will never vanish.

Shipping of both imports and exports shows no signs of lessening in the twenty-first century. As ports expand to meet these needs, they are also expanding to meet the growing demands of the cruise industry. Despite the temporary crippling effects of COVID-19, the cruise industry is flourishing as demand is being satisfied. New and larger ships are being built, providing more rooms for more passengers and creating a need for more workers on board and dockside.

Recreational boating and sportfishing continue to grow. While providing entertainment, these pastimes create jobs for thousands of workers. Commercial fishing also continues to be important along the coasts of Florida. Regulatory agencies are vigilant in managing fish populations and avoiding the risk of overfishing. Responsible commercial anglers understand these needs, and fish populations are being protected to ensure availability well into the future.

Our continuing relationship with maritime resources is crucial for Florida. While Florida is known as the "Sunshine State," it could just as easily be called the "Maritime State."

SOURCES

Christy, David. *Cotton Is King; Or, the Culture of Cotton, and Its Relation to Agriculture, Manufactures and Commerce: To the Free Colored People; and to Those Who Hold That Slavery Is in Itself Sinful.* Cincinnati, OH: American Antiquarian Society, 1855.

Dodd, Dorothy. "The Wrecking Business on the Florida Reef, 1822–1860." *Florida Historical Quarterly* 22, no. 4 (April 1944): 171–99.

Fishburne, Charles C., Jr. *The Cedar Keys.* Cedar Key, FL: Privately printed, 1982.

Florida Historical Society Quarterly 8, no. 1 (July 1929): 47–63.

Garnett, Thomas A. *Economic Effects of the 1918 Influenza Pandemic: Implications for a Modern-Day Pandemic.* St. Louis, MO: Federal Reserve Bank of St. Louis, 2007.

George, Paul S. "Brokers, Binders, and Builders: Greater Miami's Boom of the Mid-1920s." *Florida Historical Quarterly* 65, no. 1 (July 1986): 27–51.

Hammond, E.A. "Wreckers and Wrecking on the Florida Reef, 1829–1832." *Florida Historical Quarterly* 41, no. 3 (January 1963): 239–73.

Hopwood, Fred A. *The Golden Era of Steamboating on the Indian River, 1877–1900.* Cocoa: Florida Historical Society Press, 1998.

Knetsch, Joe, and Pamela Gibson. *Florida in World War I.* Charleston, SC: The History Press, 2021.

Noll, Steven, and David Tegeder. *Ditch of Dreams: The Cross Florida Barge Canal and the Struggle for Florida's Future.* Gainesville: University Press of Florida, 2009.

Palmer, Dewey H. "Moving North: Migration of Negroes During World War I." *Phylon* 28, no. 1 (1967): 52–62.

Pelt, Peggy Dorton. "Wainwright Shipyard: The Impact of a World War II War Industry on Panama City, Florida." Dissertation, Florida State University, 1994.

Stronge, William B. *Sunshine Economy: An Economic History of Florida Since the Civil War*. Gainesville: University Press of Florida, 2008.

Taylor, Robert A. "The Frogmen in Florida: U.S. Navy Combat Demolition Training in Fort Pierce, 1943–1946." *Florida Historical Quarterly* 75, no. 3 (Winter 1997): 289–302.

Wynne, Lewis N. "Shipbuilding in Tampa During World War II." *Sunland Tribune* 16, no. 13 (1990). https://digitalcommons.usf.edu/cgi/viewcontent.cgi?article=1214&context=sunlandtribune.

Wynne, Nick, and Joe Crankshaw. *Florida Civil War Blockades: Battling for the Coast*. Charleston, SC: The History Press, 2011.

Wynne, Nick, and Richard Moorhead. *Florida in World War II: Floating Fortress*. Charleston, SC: The History Press, 2010.

———. *Paradise for Sale: Florida's Booms and Busts*. Charleston, SC: The History Press, 2010.

ABOUT THE AUTHORS

NICK WYNNE (*left*) is a retired historian who lives along the shore of the Indian River Lagoon. He is also the author of numerous books, including novels about the rural South. He is a graduate of the University of Georgia.

ROBERT REDD (*center*) is a native Floridian with a longtime interest in history. He holds degrees from Stetson University and American Public University. He is a member of the Florida Historical Society, Southern Historical Society, American Battlefield Trust and other organizations. He is honored to be a part of this team in telling the story of Florida's maritime history.

JOE KNETSCH (*right*) is a graduate of Florida State University and the author of multiple books on Florida history. He retired from the Florida Department of Natural Resources and now serves as an expert witness in court cases involving land usage and navigable water rights. He is an in-demand speaker for various historical groups.

Visit us at
www.historypress.com